Fifty Lessons on Principles of Belief for Youths

Ayatullah Naser
Makarim Shirazi

Copyright

Copyright © 2022 al-Burāq Publications.

All rights reserved. No part of this publication may be reproduced, distributed, or transmitted in any form or by any means, including photocopying, recording, or other electronic or mechanical methods, without the prior written permission of the publisher, except in the case of brief quotations embodied in critical reviews and certain other noncommercial uses permitted by copyright law. For permission requests, write to the publisher, addressed "Attention: Permissions [Fifty Lessons on Principles of Belief for Youths]," at the email address below.

ISBN: 978-1-956276-06-0

Printed and published by al-Burāq Publications.

Ordering Information

We offer discounts and promotions for wholesale purchases and for non-profit organizations, libraries, and other educational institutions. Contact us at the email below for further information.

www.al-Buraq.org
publications@al-Buraq.org

First edition | February 2021
Second edition | January 2022

Dedication

The publication of this book was made possible through the generous support of our donors.

Please recite *Sūrah al-Fātiha* and ask Allāh for the Divine reward (*thawāb*) to be conferred upon the donors and also the souls of all the deceased in whose memory their loved ones have contributed graciously towards the publication of *Fifty Lessons on Principles of Belief for Youths*.

Duaa al-Hujja

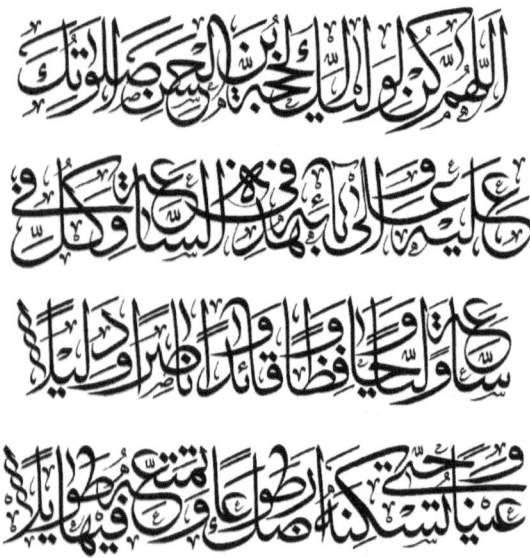

O Allah, be, for Your representative, the Hujjat (proof), son of al-Hasan, Your blessings be upon him and his forefathers, in this hour and in every hour: a guardian, a protector, a leader, a helper, a proof, and an eye - until You make him live on the Earth, in obedience (to You), and cause him to live in it for a long time.

Table of Contents

Preface 1

Prelude 5

Lesson 1: Why Do We Think About God and Study Ways of Knowing the Creator of the Universe? 8

Lesson 2: The Signs of God in Our Daily Life 13

Lesson 3: Two Clear Ways of Knowing God 19

Lesson 4: An Answer to an Important Question 24

Lesson 5: A True Story 29

Lesson 6: The Second Way of Coming to Know God .. 33

Lesson 7: Examples From Creation 37

Lesson 8: A World of Wonder in a Small Bird 43

Lesson 9: Love for Insects and Flowers 47

Lesson 10: In the World of Infinitely Small Things 52

Lesson 11: What is Justice? 63

Lesson 12: Proof or Reason for The Creator's Justice. 70

Lesson 13: The Philosophy of Signs and Evil 76

Lesson 14: The Philosophy of Undesirable Events in Life 83

Lesson 15: Once Again the Philosophy of Signs and Catastrophes 88

Lesson 16: The Issue of Predestination & Free Will 95

Lesson 17: The Clearest Reason for Free Will 102

Lesson 18: A World of Wonder in a Small Bird: What is the 'Middle Way'? 108

Lesson 19: Guidance and Error are in God's Hands..115

Lesson 20: God's Justice and the Issue of Eternity....121

Lesson 21: Our Need for Divine Leaders 127

Lesson 22: The Need of having Prophets who Present The Law 135

Lesson 23: Why are the Prophets Free of Sin and Error? 143

Lesson 24: The Best Way to come to Know the Prophets 149

Lesson 25: The Greatest Miracle of the Prophef of Islam 157

Lesson 26: A Glance at the Miracle of the Qur'an 164

Lesson 27: The World View of the Holy Qur'an.........170

Lesson 28: The Holy Qur'an and Modern Scientific Discoveries 177

Lesson 29: Another Proof of the Rightfulness of the Prophet of Islam 183

Lesson 30: The Prophet of Islam is the "Seal of Prophecy" 191

Lesson 31: When did Imamology Begin?....................200

Lesson 32: The Philosophy of the Existence of Imams (Guides)..207

Lesson 33: The Conditions and Special Qualities of the Imam 214

Lesson 34: Who has to Select the Imam? 221

Lesson 35: The Qur'an and Imamate 231

Lesson 36: Imamate in the Traditions of the Holy Prophet 240

Lesson 37: The Tradition of Manzalah and the Tradition of Yawm Ad-Dar 248

Lesson 38: The Tradition of Thaqalayn and Noah"s Ark 254

Lesson 39: The Twelve Imams 261

Lesson 40: The Twelfth Imam, The Great Leader and Peace-Maker of the World 269

Lesson 41: One Crucial Question: Is Death considered as One"s End or Beginning? 280

Lesson 42: Belief in The Resurrection Gives Meaning to Life 287

Lesson 43: An Example of the Trial of the Day of Judgment is within You 294

Lesson 44: Belief in Resurrection is Manifested in our Primordial Nature 299

Lesson 45: The Resurrection & the Scales of Justice . 305

Lesson 46: We Have Seen the Resurrection Many Times in this World 310

Lesson 47: The Resurrection and The Philosophy of Creation 316

Lesson 48: The Survival of the Spirit, a Sign of the Resurrection 323

Lesson 49: The Physical-Spiritual Resurrection 327

Lesson 50: Paradise and Hell are the Embodiment of our Deeds..335

Preface

*In the Name of Allāh, the Most Gracious,
the Most Merciful*

The precious legacy left behind by the Holy Prophet's Household [Ahl al-Bayt] (may peace be upon them all) and their followers' preservation of this legacy from the menace of extinction is a perfect example of the all-encompassing school [madrasah] that embraces all the different branches of Islamic knowledge.

This school has been able to train many talented personalities by quenching them with this gushing fountain. This school has given scholars to the Muslim ummah who, by following the Holy Prophet's Household (a.s), have done their best in order to clear away the doubts and skepticisms put forth by any various creeds and intellectual currents both inside and outside Muslim society. Throughout past centuries, they have presented the firmest answers and solutions to these doubts.

Anchored to the responsibilities upon its shoulders, the Ahl al-Bayt (a.s) World Assembly has embarked on defending the sanctity of risalah [message] and its authentic beliefs—truths which have always been opposed by the chiefs and leaders of anti-Islamic sects, religions and trends.

In this sacred path, the Assembly regards itself as a follower of the upright pupils of the School of the Ahl al-Bayt (a.s)—those who have always been ready to refute those accusations and calumnies and have tried to be always in the frontline of this struggle on the basis of the expediencies of time and space.

The experiences in this field, which contained the books of scholars belonging to the School of the Ahl al-Bayt (a.s), are unique in their own right. It is because these experiences have been based upon knowledge [`ilm] and the preeminence of intellect and reasoning, and at the same time, they are devoid of blind prejudices or whims and caprices. These experiences address experts, scholars and thinkers in a manner that appeals to healthy minds and pure human natural disposition [fitrah].

In a bid to assist those who are in quest of truth, the Ahl al-Bayt (a.s) World Assembly has endeavored to enter a new phase of these worthy experiences by conducting research and translating the works of contemporary Shi`ah writers or those who, through divine guidance, have embraced this noble school.

The Assembly is also engaged in the study and publication of the valuable works of pious predecessors and outstanding Shi`ah personalities so that those who search for the truth may quench their thirst from this palatable fountain which the School of the Prophet's Household (a.s) offers to the entire world.

It is hoped that the dear readers will not deprive the Ahl al-Bayt (a.s) World Assembly of their valuable opinions, suggestions, and constructive criticisms in this arena.

We also invite scholars, translators and other institutions to assist us in propagating pure Muhammadan (s) Islam.

We ask God, the Exalted, to accept this humble effort and enhance it further under the auspices of His vicegerent on earth and give us success with al-Mahdi (may Allah, the Exalted, expedite his glorious advent).

It is appropriate here to express our utmost gratitude to Ayatullah Makarim Shirazi for writing the book and to Dr. Mahmoud Farrokhpey for translating this work. We should also like to thank colleagues who took part in accomplishing this task especially the staff of the Translation Office for fulfilling their responsibility.

Cultural Affairs Department

The Ahl al-Bayt (a.s) World Assembly

Prelude

The most salient feature of our Islamic revolution is its Islamic nature and the most prominent characteristic of Islam is its personality building aspect based on Divine standards.

Our aim is to prepare an interesting, logic-based and rigorous collection of papers for the general public on the one hand, and for the youth in particular so that they could, under existing Islamic conditions, build a sturdy faith which could in the long run influence their behavior and also be used as an impetus for further studies.

This collection which has been prepared with special precision and initiatives could pave the way for those who need to acquire the Islamic principles on faith for both their personal interests or for instruction.

This collection has been written and prepared by Ayatullah Nasir Makarim Shirazi, a profound pioneer and initiator of religious discussions in the Qom Seminary for the last forty years.

The instructors who wish to teach these lectures to their students should make note of the following points:

Fifty Lessons on Principles of Belief for Youths

1. These lessons should be accompanied with historic evidence and interesting observations based on current affairs.

2. The students' preferences and previous knowledge should be considered in teaching these lessons. A question and answer approach should be used during instruction.

3. The relevant Qur'anic verses on which the lecture is based should be elegantly written on the board and the students should be presented with a literal translation of the verse under consideration. This will lay the foundation for their familiarity with the Holy Qur'an. It is recommended that the relevant verse be recited by one and repeated by the students in unison.

4. If it is not necessary to cover one lecture in one sitting: it could be covered within two sessions.

5. There are subtle and detailed points hidden in each lecture. The lecturer is well advised to study the lecture beforehand in order to bring up those points during the presentation.

6. These lectures are prepared for the students of junior-high school and high school, for both boys and girls, and for the general public who wish to

improve their knowledge of the principles of the Islamic faith.

7. Giving prizes to those who successfully pass the exams based on these lectures is highly recommended.

8. Students who are exposed to these lectures might have some theological questions in mind. The following sources could be used as references in order to arrive at appropriate answers: "The Creator of the Universe," "In search of Allah," and "Religious Questions and Answers."

Lesson 1: Why Do We Think About God and Study Ways of Knowing the Creator of the Universe?

The Love to be Informed About and Know the World is Deep Inside Every One of Us We all want to know, in truth: Did this elevated heaven, with its beautiful stars, this extensive earth, with its heart-rendering views; these various creatures; beautiful birds; various kinds of fish, the seas and flowers; the blossoms, plants, abundant trees, whose tops reach towards the heavens; did all of these things come into being of their own free will or were all of these wonderful forms painted by an expert, a powerful painter?

Beyond all of this, the first question which comes to mind for all of us is: Where did we come from? Where are we? Where are we going? If we know the answers to these three questions, how happy will we be! That is, if we know where our life began and where it will finally end and what duties we have now, our searching spirit tells us: you must not sit quietly until the answers come.

It often happens that in an automobile accident, a person is injured and becomes unconscious and for his treatment, they take him to a hospital. When his condition has improved a bit, and when he awakens, the first thing which he asks of those around him is: "Where am I? Why did you bring me here? When can I leave here?" All of these questions show that a person cannot remain indifferent and not ask these questions.

Thus, the first thing which sends us looking for God and understanding of the creation of the world of existence is our very thirsty spirit of search.

A Sense of Thankfulness

Pretend that you have been invited to a very important affair and all means of convenience have been provided for you but, because you have been invited through your brother, you do not know the host well. The first thing you will want to do when you enter the gathering is to find the host to thank him.

When we look at this widespread created world and the multiple blessings which have been provided for us: eyes which see, ears which hear, sufficient intelligence, various physical and psychological abilities, various means for living and for earning our livelihood, we automatically begin to think about trying to know He Who has given us all of these blessings and even though He does not need our thanks, we still thank Him and, until we do this, we are unhappy with ourselves and feel we have not done a duty.

This is another reason why we begin to search to come to know God.

The Bond Between Things to our Benefit and Things to Our Harm with this Example

Pretend that we are going on a journey and we reach a cross-road in which there is a great deal of commotion. Everyone warns us not to stop at this cross-road because there is great danger there. Each group invites us to go its way. One group says, "The best way is to go east.

Another says, "Go West. It is the best road." The third group invites us to a road or a way which is between the other two, saying, "This is the only way of saving yourself from danger and reaching your home safely. This is the way that will give you happiness and security and be a place of refuge for you."

Would we allow ourselves to choose a way without study? Will our mind allow us to stop there and not choose any way? Clearly not.

Rather, our mind and our wisdom tells us to begin immediately to study and research, to listen to the words of each group carefully and accept whichever way has the most correct signs, speaks the truth and has convincing reasons for taking that way. Having assured ourselves of the right way, we take it and move forward.

In life in this world, also, we have such a condition. Different religions and schools of thought invite us to take their way, but as our fate, our fortune and misfortune, our progress and backwardness depends upon our study and making the best choice, we are obliged to think about this and prevent ourselves from falling into misfortune, corruption and difficulties.

This is yet another reason which invites us to search for the Creator of the world. The Holy Qur'an says:

"So give good tidings to my servants, those who listen to the sayings and follow the best of it..." (39:18)

Think and Answer
1. Other than what your mother and father have told you about God, have you seriously thought about Him?

2. Can you say what the difference is between 'searching for God' and 'knowing God'?

3. Have you ever felt a deep sense of spiritual love for God when you have whispered your prayers to Him?

Lesson 2: The Signs of God in Our Daily Life

Knowing God and the Progress of Science

Pretend that a friend has come from a trip and has brought a book as a present for you. He says that it is an excellent book, because the author of this book is full of information by a very great scholar, who is accurate, an expert and a genius in his own field.

You will most certainly not study this book carelessly. Rather you will concentrate on every sentence and even the choice of words made and if there be a sentence there that you do not understand, perhaps you will spend hours and even days, whenever you can, studying it until the meaning of it becomes clear to you.

Why? Because the author of this book is not a normal average person but rather a great scholar who considers every word he uses carefully.

But if the opposite were true and they had said to you, "This book may appear to be beautiful and pleasing on the outside, but the author is not very literate and he has no base in science and has not taken any care," it is clear that you will only quickly glance at the book and wherever you found something unclear in it, you would say, "This is because the author was uninformed and it is a waste of time for a person to study this."

The world of creation is like a great book in which every creature forms a word or sentence in that. From the point of view of a person who worships God, every atom of this universe is worthy of study.

A person who has faith in the ray of the light of worshiping God, will make use of a special sense of curiosity in studying the secrets of creation and it is this very fact which helps science and human knowledge to progress - because he knows that the Creator of this universe has endless knowledge and power and everything He does is based on a wisdom and a philosophy. Thus, he studies with greater care, more profoundly in order to be able to understand the secrets better.

But a materialist has no reason to discover the secret of creation for he believes that nature is senseless. If we look at the work of a materialist scholar, it is in the same rank because he accepts God but calls him 'nature'. Why? Because he accepts an order and a program in nature.

Knowing God, Endeavoring and Hope

Whenever a difficult and complicated event takes place in the life of a human being, whenever all doors are somehow closed, one senses weakness, hopelessness and loneliness, when confronted by these difficulties, a person with faith in God then seeks His help, which He gives.

A person who has faith in God does not see himself or herself as being alone or powerless. He or she does not despair. He or she does not sense weakness or inability, because God is above all difficulties and everything is easy for Him.

With hope in His kindness, support and help, he or she will struggle against the difficulty and will use all of his or her energies. With love and hope, one will continue his or her endeavors and efforts and will overcome the difficulty.

Yes. Faith in God is a great place of refuge for a human being. Faith in God is the substance of perseverance and steadfastness. Faith in God always keeps hope in hearts alive. Because of this, individuals with faith never attempt to commit suicide because attempts at suicide come from despair, a complete lack of hope and a feeling of having failed but individuals with faith neither lose hope nor do they sense failure.

Knowing God and the Sense of Responsibility

We know a doctor who, when poor people visit him, not only does he not get money from them for the visit, but he gives them money and drugs and if he senses a danger for that person, he will stay all night in his home. These are people who worship God and have faith.

But we also know a doctor who, until the money of the visit is not paid, he will not take the first step for the sick person because he does not have a strong faith. A person who has faith, no matter what his or her profession is, senses responsibility, knows his or her duties, does good, readily forgives and constantly sees a spiritual policeman within his or her soul who watches over one's deeds.

But people who lack faith are selfish and dangerous people who have no sense of responsibility. Oppression, suppression and aggression against the rights of others is easy for them and they are less prepared to do good.

Knowing God and Peacefulness

Psychologists say that mental and psychological diseases are greater in our time than in any other. They say that one of the factors is anxiety over future events, anxiety over death, anxiety over war and anxiety of fear and failure.

They add, "Among the things which can take anxiety away from a person's spirit is faith in god because whenever an anxiety wants to penetrate one's spirit, faith in God pushes it away."

A God who is kind, a God who helps one meet one's needs, a God Who is aware of His servants' condition and if they turn towards Him, He helps them and frees them from anxiety.

Because of this, a real believer always has a sense of peacefulness and no anxiety exists within his or her spirit. Whatever such a person does, is for God. Even if one suffers a loss, one seeks its replacement from Him. Such a person even enters the war front with a smile.

The Holy Qur'an says:

"It is those who believe and confuse not their beliefs with oppression — that are (truly) in peacefulness, for they are on (right) guidance." (6:82)

Think and Answer

1. Do you recall the fate of the people in the past which the Qur'anic verse refers to?

2. Do you know why some individuals, who pretend to have faith in God, are morally corrupt and none of the four effects mentioned above can be found in them?

Lesson 3: Two Clear Ways of Knowing God

From the earliest of times until today, books have been written about coming to know God and a great deal has been said by scholars and non-scholars.

Each one chooses a way in order to come to understand this issue but from among all of the ways, there are two ways which can help us to grow near to this great Creator of the universe:

•First, an inward way (the closest way)

•Second, an outward way (the clearest way)

With the first way, we get in touch with our deep inner self and we hear the cry of monotheism from within the depths of ourselves.

With the second way, we explore the expansive created world, and we see the signs of the creator in all creatures and in the heart of every atom. Each one of these two ways requires a great deal of explanation, but what we will try to do is to briefly study each of these two ways.

The Inward Way

Let us think about the following:

Scholars say that every human being who thinks, from whatever class or race one be, if left alone, receives no special training, not even hears the words of people who worship God nor the words of materialists, that person will naturally become aware of a force or power which is above nature and which rules all of the world.

In the corners of one's heart and spirit, one will sense a very subtle sound, which is full of kindness and, at the same time, clear and firm, which calls one towards the great Source of the universe and the power that we call God. This is that very pure, divinely-created human nature of people.

It is possible that one becomes occupied with the commotion in the material world and one's daily life and the lights and attractions of life and one may temporarily neglect to hear this sound, but when one finds oneself facing problems and difficulties, whenever a natural catastrophe like a flood or an earthquake or a hurricane comes, yes, at this time, when one is curtailed from all means of material life, and when one finds no place of refuge, this inner sound gains strength.

Lesson 3

One senses that within one's self, a power is calling one, a power which is superior to all forces, a secret force and all difficulties and problems seem simple before it.

It is rare to find a person who in such difficulties does not automatically turn to God. It is this issue which shows how close we are to Him and how close He is to us.

He is in our spirit and our very soul. Of course, the cry of instinct (nature) is always within a person, but at times like this, it finds greater force.

Our history shows that even the powerful rulers who, at the time of peace and calm, refuse to even mention the Name of God, when the bases of their power begin to shake and they see that they are about to lose all of their power, they turn to God and they hear the voice of their Divinely-created nature.

History tells us that when Pharaoh saw that he was drowning in the waves of the sea, he said, "I confess that there is no god but the great God of Moses." This cry came from his soul. Not only Pharaoh, but all people who are in a state or condition like he was, cry out the same thing he did.

If you study the real reasons for this, you will agree that a light shines from there which calls you to God. Perhaps there have been times when you have met with difficulties and problems and all of the usual ways of solving problems do not work. At that moment, most certainly, you have seen that there is a force in the world which can easily solve it.

At this moment, a hope mixed with love fills your spirit and soul and it removes the clouds of darkness from our soul. Yes. This is the closest way which a person can take to God.

Only one question:

We know that this question may arise for some of you. Does this possibility not exist that based upon what we have been taught by our environment, our father and mother, at sensitive moments, we begin to think that we should ask God for help?

We know you are right and correct in asking this question, but we have a very interesting answer which we give in the next lesson.

The Holy Qur'an says:

Lesson 3

"Now, if they embark on a boat, they call on God, making their devotion sincerely (and exclusively) to Him; but when He has delivered them safely to (dry) land, behold, they give a Share (of their worship to others)!" (29:65)

Think and Answer

1. Try to memorize the surah number, verse number and meaning of word to word translation and gradually become familiar with the language of the Holy Qur'an.

2. Has a complicated problem ever arisen for you for which no solution seemed available to you except the kindness of God, the Almighty? (Write or tell about it briefly).

3. Why is this way called the closest way?

Lesson 4: An Answer to an Important Question

Question: In the previous lesson, we realized or recognized that we always hear the voice of monotheism (tawhid) and worship of God from within our souls and especially at times of difficulty, this voice becomes stronger and clearer and we naturally begin to think about God and we seek His help and kindness.

Here it is possible that this question arises that this inner voice which we call the voice of our God-given nature (fitrat) is the result of things which we have heard from our environment and our mother and father have told us or from school and it has become very normal and common for us.

Answer: The answer to this requires a brief introduction. Customs change. We cannot find a custom which has not changed throughout history among all nations.

Thus, when we see that this is something which exists among all nations, has existed at all times and during all ages, without exception, we should realize that its roots are in fitrat and that it is woven into the spirit and soul of human beings.

Lesson 4

For instance, the love of a mother for her child. This can in no way be said to come from propaganda or habit or custom because in no tribe or nation, or at any time or age, can you see that a mother does not love her child.

Of course, it is possible that a mother, because of a mental disturbance, do away with herself or a father during the Age of Ignorance in Arabia (the time before the appearance of Islam) buried his girl children alive because his thoughts were wrong and based on superstitions but these are very rare cases.

Looking at this introduction, recalling how people in the past and in the present worship God, we see (as this lesson is a little bit more difficult, please pay careful attention).

As stated by sociologists and historians, there has been no time in history when belief in God and faith did not exist among people. Rather, in every age and time and at all moments of this world, some form of belief existed and this, itself, is clear reason why the worship of God is from the depths of the spirit and its source is fitrat of human beings, not that it is a result of customs we have accepted because if it were the consequences of habit and custom, it would not be so extensive and eternal.

We even have rules which show that tribes who lived before written history began, had some kind of a belief system. Of course, there is no doubt that at times, when people had forgotten God as the Being Who is above nature, they searched for Him and looked for Him among creatures in nature and they made idols for themselves of things in nature.

But with the development of thought, human beings gradually were able to see the truth, stop worshipping idols which were material creatures and become familiar with the One God.

Some of the well-known psychologists clearly and directly say that the human spirit or soul has four senses:

First, the sense of knowledge which sends a person after science and knowledge and makes one's spirit thirsty for knowledge whether or not this has any material benefit.

Second, the sense of goodness which is the source for moral and human issues in the world of humanity.

Third, the sense of beauty which is the source of poetry and literature and art in their real sense.

Fourth, the sense of belief which invites the human being to come to know God and to implement His Commands. In this way, we see that the sense of worship is one of the senses with the deepest roots of the spirit. That is, they are never separate from each other.

In our future lessons, we will see how most materialists even admit to the existence of God, even though they do not mention His Name and instead refer to nature or give Him other names but qualities are given to nature which are, in fact, qualities of God.

For instance, they say, if nature has given two kidneys to human beings, it was because it knew that if one of these failed, the other would continue life, etc.

Does this explanation hold for a nature which lacks awareness and consciousness? Or is this not a reference to the All-knowing and Infinite God but calling Him, nature?

We can conclude from what has been said that:

A love for God has always existed in us and will always continue.

Faith in God is an eternal flame which warms our heart and spirit.

In order to come to know God, we are not obliged to take a long and complicated way.

We quickly turn inward and see we have faith in Him. The Holy Qur'an says:

"We are closer to the human being than his jugular vein."
(50:16)

Think and Answer

1. Write several examples of customs and several examples of things which are part of our God-given nature (fitrat).

2. Why do ignorant people turn to idol worship?

3. Why do materialists refer to God as Nature?

Lesson 5: A True Story

We have said that in the depths of the spirit of those who deny God with their tongue, a faith in God exists.

There is no doubt that victories and successes — especially for individuals with few possibilities develop pride and this very pride becomes the source for forgetfulness, to the point where often a person even forgets his or her own opinions.

But the moment that a storm of difficulties throws their life into chaos and the strong wind of difficulties attacks that person from all sides, the curtains of pride and selfishness moves away from their eyes and divinely-created nature (fitrat) and monotheism (the belief that God is One) appears.

History gives many examples of individuals who were like this, whose lives were full of deceit:

There was a minister who was very strong and powerful in his age. He had taken control of most of the power and no one opposed him. One day he entered a meeting in which a group of religious scholars were present. He turned to them and said, "For how long will you continue to say that God exists? I have many reasons to prove otherwise."

He said this with special pride. As the scholars who were present knew that he was not a reasonable or logical person and that power and strength had made him so proud that no words of truth would affect him, they ignored him and remained silent, a meaningful and humble silence.

This event passed. After a time, the minister insulted someone. The ruler of the time had him arrested and thrown into jail.

One of the scholars who were present at the gathering thought to himself that the time to awaken him had come.

Now that he has gotten off the horse of pride and the curtain of self-interest has moved away from his eyes, and the sense of accepting the truth was awakened in him, if he contacts him and gives him words of advice, it may produce good results. He received permission to visit him and he went to the prison.

As he neared him, he saw that he was in a room all alone, walking back and forth and thinking and he was recalling a poem which said, "We are all like drawings or paintings of a lion which are painted or drawn on a flag. When the wind blows, it moves and perhaps even attacks, but in reality it has nothing from itself. Its strength is the wind which gives it power. We, also, as we gain more power, have nothing from ourselves. It is God who has given this strength to us and whenever He wills, He can take it from us."

The above-mentioned scholar saw that under these conditions, not only does he not deny the existence of God, but he has become ardently aware of God. After greeting him he said, "Do you recall how you said you have many reasons for the non-existence of God.

I have come to answer those many reasons with just one response, "God is He Who, with such ease, took your power away from you." He hung his head in shame and did not answer because he knew that he had been wrong and he saw the light of God within himself.

The Holy Qur'an says:

"We took the Israeli tribes across the sea; Pharaoh and his hosts followed them in pride and insolence. At length, when overwhelmed with the flood, he said, "I believe that there is no god except Him whom the Israeli tribes believe in. I am of those who submit (muslimin)" " (10:90)

Think and Answer

1. Describe the consequences of the true story in several lines.

2. Why are the Israeli tribe called "Israeli tribe"?

3. Who was Pharaoh? Where did he live? What claims did he make?

Lesson 6: The Second Way of Coming to Know God

The Outer Way

With a quick glance at the world that we live in, we realize that the world is not in chaos and disorder. Rather, all phenomena are in motion moving towards a clear and determined direction. The facilities of the world are like a great army which has been divided into well-organized units which move in a determined direction.

The following points will clarify any ambiguities:

1. In order to come into being and to remain, every living creature must be a part of a series of laws and special conditions. For instance, for a tree to be, water and suitable soil and a specific temperature are necessary for us to plant seeds and nourish them and each seed to become green and grow. If these conditions do not exist, there is no possibility for growth and the choosing of these conditions and proving the necessary preliminaries requires an intellect and knowledge.

2. Every creature has a special effect which is exclusive to it. Water and fire each have their own particularities which do not separate from them and they constantly follow permanent laws.

3. All of the members (organs) of living creatures work and are coordinated with each other. As an example, this very human body, which is itself a world, all works together consciously and unconsciously in a special coordination. For instance, if a danger arises, all are mobilized for defense. This relationship and cooperation is another sign of the order in the universe.

4. One look at the world scene makes it clear that not only are all organs of one body of one living creature in coordination with each other, but all the various creatures of the world are also in special coordination with each other. For instance, for the nourishment of living creatures, the sun shines, clouds bring rain and the earth and resources of the earth also help. This all shows the existence of one clear system in the universe.

The Relationship of Order and Intellect

This truth is clear for everyone's conscience that whenever order exists in a facility, this shows intellect, thought, a plan and a goal.

Because whenever a human being sees order, permanent laws and a reckoning of things, he or she knows that beside that source, knowledge and power must also be sought and in understanding this, in one's conscience, he or she does not see need for reasoning.

He or she knows that a blind person or an illiterate person can never type a good essay or write a social or critical article, that a child of two years old can never paint beautiful and valuable painting by the drawing of lines on a piece of paper.

Rather, if we see a good essay or read a good article, we know that a person who is literate or if we have seen very beautiful paintings, we will have no doubt that an expert painted them even if we have never met or seen that painter.

Thus, wherever there is a sense of order, beside that, there has been an intellect and however much larger that system be, it is more accurate and more interesting, the knowledge which brings that into being in the same proportion is greater.

Sometimes, in order to prove this issue that every system needs a source of knowledge, the law of probabilities, which has been achieved in high mathematics is used to prove that, for instance, if an illiterate individual wants to type an article or an essay or a poem by randomly pressuring on the keys of the machine, according to the law of probabilities, this will take millions of years to attain for which one lifetime is not sufficient.

The Holy Qur'an says:

"Soon will We show them Our Signs upon the horizons and in their own souls, until it becomes manifest to them that this is the Truth. Is it not enough that Thy Nourisher is aware of all things." (41:53)

Think and Answer

1. Give a few examples (other than those presented in the story) about industrial units, the observation of which shows the existence of a Creator of the world Who is Aware.

2. What is the difference between 'horizons' and 'souls'? Give examples of God in the 'horizons' and within one's own 'soul'.

Lesson 7: Examples From Creation

Throughout the world, 'order', 'goal' and 'design' are apparent. Now pay attention as we study some examples of this. We will present some large and small examples for you.

Fortunately, today, with the progress made in natural sciences, the discovery of the secrets and wonders of the world of nature, and the subtleties in the existence of human beings, animals and plants, the wonderful structure of a cell or an atom and the wonderful system of the stars, the doors of knowing God have been opened to us in such a way that one can clearly say that all books of natural science are books about the oneness and unity of God which teach us great lessons about the great Creator because these books remove the veils or curtains which cover the interesting order of the creatures of this world and show how important the Creator of this world is.

The center of administration of the country of your body

Our skull has been filled with grey matter called the brain. This brain forms the most accurate and exact system of our body because it commands all of the powers of our body and it manages all of the organs of our system.

In order to understand the importance of this great center, it would be a good idea for us to explain the following for you.

The newspapers had printed that a Shiraz university student in Khuzistan was in an automobile accident and his brain was damaged but it seemed that nothing at all had happened to him. All of his organs were healthy but strangely enough, he had forgotten all of his past life. His mind worked well.

He could study but if he saw his mother and father, he did not recognize them. When they said to him that this was his mother, he was surprised. They took him to his home in Shiraz. They showed him the handicraft work he had done and then hung on the walls of his room.

But he looked at it all in amazement and said that he was seeing these things for the first time.

It became clear that in the brain damage he suffered, cells which were, in reality, transitions between thought and his memory were no longer working and like a blown out fuse which cuts off the electricity and brings darkness, his memory of the past had been disconnected.

Lesson 7

Perhaps the point which no longer works is no bigger than the size of the top of a pin but what an effect it has had upon his life and from this it becomes clear how complicated and how important our brain is.

Our brain consists of two separate parts: first, the part which is controlled by our voluntary which controls all of our voluntary motions like walking, looking, speaking.

Second, the involuntary part which controls the movement of our heart, stomach, etc. and if one part of this part of the brain does not function, the heart or another organ will no longer function.

One of the Most Wonderful Parts of the Brain

The cerebrum is the center of will power, consciousness and memory. In other words, it is one of the most sensitive areas of the brain and many of the reactions of the inner senses like anger, fear, etc. relate to it.

If we take out the cerebrum in an animal but we leave the other organs as they are, it will remain alive but its understanding and consciousness will be totally eliminated.

They have removed the brain of a pigeon. It remained alive for a while but it could not eat seeds that were placed in front of it. Even though it was hungry, it would not eat.

If it was allowed to fly, it flew until it hit a barrier and fell down.

Another Wonderful Part of the Brain is the Sense of Memory

Have you ever thought how wonderful our sense of memory is? If our sense of memory is taken from us for even one hour, what a difficult situation we will be placed in.

The center of memory which forms a small part of our brain is where all of our memories of our lifetime are stored. Whoever is related to us, the particularities of that person as to size, form, color, clothes and spirit, are kept in storage in their own area and a special file is formed for each one.

Thus the moment we confront that person, our mind removes him from the file and immediately, completely reviews what we know about him and then it commands us as to what reaction we should have.

If it is a friend, respect and if it is an enemy, the showing of hatred but all of this is done so quickly that there is more or less no lapse of time.

The wonder of this becomes more apparent when we try to recall what is stored and draw it or write it down or record it in a tape recorder.

Without any doubt, it will require a great deal of paper or a great number of tapes which can fill a large storage room.

Even more wonderful than this is when we want to find one drawing or one tape among them, a file clerk will be necessary but our sense of memory does all of this work very simply, easily and quickly.

How can an Unconscious nature create a conscious one?

Many books have been written about the wonders of the human brain. Can you believe that such an extraordinary system which is so subtle, accurate, complicated and mysterious be made from unconscious nature?

More wonderful than this is to believe that an unintelligent nature could create intelligence!

The Holy Qur'an says:

"On the earth are signs for those of assured faith as also in your own selves: will you not then see?"(51:21)

Think and Answer

1. Do you have any other information about the wonders of the human brain?

2. What has God created in order to protect the human brain against accident?

Lesson 8: A World of Wonder in a Small Bird

In this lesson, we want to leave aside the large country of our body, which we have only very briefly touched upon, and turn to a look at the wonderful order of other creatures.

We look at the sky in the darkness of night. We see an exceptional bird which is searching for food with all of its energy. This bird is a bat. There are many wondrous things but flying at night is among the most wondrous.

The swift flight of bats in the darkness of the night without hitting anything is so wondrous that no matter how often one studies this, new mysteries of this are revealed.

This bird flies with the same speed and accuracy as a pigeon does in the day time. If it flies into a dark and narrow tunnel which is full of smoke and twists and turns, it will fly through all of the twists and turns without hitting any of the walls and not the smallest amount of smoke will be found on its wings.

This strange ability of the bat is proof of an effect within it which is similar to radar. We now need to know what radar is in order to be able to see it in a small bat.

In physics, in the discussion on forms, waves are discussed which are beyond sound waves. These waves are those same waves whose length and frequency are so great that the human ear cannot hear them. This is why they are called meta-sound waves.

When these waves are set off by means of a very strong transmitter, these waves move forward but whenever they meet up with any kind of a barrier in a point of space (like the aircraft of the enemy, etc), just like a ball when it hits a wall and bounces back, like our voice before a mountain or a high wall and based on an accurate record of how long it takes for the sound to return to us, we can measure the exact distance to the object.

Many aircrafts and ships are guided by means of radar and it takes them to whatever direction they want.

It is also used to find out the location of enemy ships and aircraft.

Scholars say that within this small creature, there is something similar to radar so that if the bat flies in a room which at that same moment a microphone is put to use to transform meta-sound waves into sound waves which can be heard, in each second (30 to 60 times) the meta-sound waves will be heard by the bat.

Scholars in answer to this say, "These waves leave the larynx through the nose of the bat by means of strong organs and its ears, which are the receivers, receive these."

Thus, this bat, in its night travels, is obligated to its ears. A scholar, through experiment, has proven that if you remove the ears of a bat, it cannot fly avoiding things whereas if you completely remove its eyes, it will very expertly still be able to fly. That is, a bat sees with its ears! Not its eyes. And this is most strange.

Now think who created these two wondrous organs in this small creature and how was it taught how to use them? And how can it avoid the dangers which exist during its night flying? Who?

Is it possible that nature have the intelligence and consciousness to do this? and place these organs which scientists copy, at great expense, in its body?

Hadrat 'Ali, peace be upon him, in the Nahj al-Balaghah, in a very long sermon about creation, mentions the bat, saying, "It is never prevented from the way because of the darkness of the night. Great and glorious is God Who, without a previous model, brought everything into being."

Think and Answer

1. What other interesting information do you have about the bat?

2. Did you know that the bat's wings and how it bears children and that even its method of sleeping differs from other animals and that it is most exceptional?

Lesson 9: Love for Insects and Flowers

One spring day when the weather is, little by little, growing warmer, make a visit to a park or a farm. You will meet up with all sorts of small insects, honey bees, flies, butterflies and mosquitoes, who, without making a sound, fly from one flower to the next and from this branch to that branch of the trees.

They are so busy with their work that one could imagine an employer is overlooking their progress and continuously telling them what to do. Their wings and feet are colored yellow by the pollen of the flowers, giving them the look of workers who have put on their work clothes and with love and seriousness, they continue their work.

In truth, they have a very important assignment which is so great that Professor Leon Briton says, "Few people realize that without the work of insects, our fruit baskets would be empty."

And we add this sentence, "The next year, our green gardens and pastures would be completely lost. Thus, insects are, in reality, the real nourishers of fruit and providers of flower seeds."

You most probably ask why. Because the most sensitive act in the life of flowers is performed with their help. You have probably heard that flowers, like many animals, have two parts, masculine and feminine, and that reproduction takes place through their union, giving us seeds and fruit.

But have you ever thought how the two parts of flowers, which do not move, are attracted to each other? And how the male spermatozoa mix with the female ovary and provide the beginning of a marriage between the two?

This work is most often the work of insects and, in some cases; it is the work of the wind. But this is not as simple as we think it is. This fruitful marriage, in which insects act as the intermediates, has a history, formality and long adventure, only a small part of which we mention here with a short story.

Two old and close friends: Natural scientists, after study, have concluded that flowers and plants appeared in the second geological age and strangely enough, insects appeared at the same time. These two, throughout the eventful history of creation, were like two old and close friends who have remained loyal to each other and have been complements to one another.

Lesson 9

Flowers have always stored sweet nectar within themselves in order to further attract and sweeten the relationship. At the time when insects enter the flower in order to transfer the masculine group, provide the preliminaries for the marriage and pregnancy, the flower freely gives of its sweetness to them. This sweet and valuable sugar is so good tasting to the insect that they are naturally pulled towards it.

Some botanists believe that the beautiful colors and good smelling perfume of flowers also play an important role in attracting the insects to them. Various experiments with honey bees have shown that they distinguish colors and the aroma of flowers.

In reality, it is these flowers which grow for insects and have a good-smelling aroma in such a way that a butterfly and honey bees are attracted to them. They accept the invitation with all of their being and quickly begin the preliminaries and eat of their sweetness.

This very sweetness is a special kind of sugar which is considered to be the best food for insects. When it is stored in one place, it makes honey because insects are attracted to flowers. It eats some of this sweetness and takes most of it with them to their honeycomb to store. This is a contract of friendship and love which is based on mutual interest, always existed and will continue to exist between flowers and insects.

A lesson about monotheism: when a human being studies these wondrous points in the lives of insects and flowers, he or she automatically asks, "Who established this pact of love and friendship between insects and flowers?"

Who gave this special sweetness and good tasting nectar to flowers? Who granted flowers these attractive colors, beauty and this sweet-smelling perfume? Who invited in sects towards it? What were the fat and tiny bodies of insects, butterflies, honey bees and golden bees given to make them prepared to collect the pollen of flowers?

Why do bees, for a certain period of time, move towards one kind of flower? Why did the life of flowers and insects begin at one time in the created world?

Can anyone - no matter how stubborn - accept the fact that all of these events were without any plan or pre-design? And the unconscious laws of nature automatically brought such wondrous scenes into being? Never!

Lesson 9

"And thy Nourisher taught the bee to build its cells in hills, on trees and in habitations then to eat of all the produce (of the earth) and find with skill the spacious paths of its Nourisher..." (16:68-69)

Think and Answer

1. What use does the sweetness, color and perfume of flowers have?

2. What do you know about the amazing life of honey bees?

Lesson 10: In the World of Infinitely Small Things

Because we are nurtured in the wondrous world of creation and we are familiar with it, we may be unaware of the importance of many of its wonders such as:

Insects and very tiny animals live around us, which if measured, would not even be two millimeters but just like large animals, they have hands, feet, eyes, ears, even brains, awareness, a certain series of nerves and digestive facilities.

If we put the brain of an ant under a microscope and if we study its amazing structure with care, we would see what a strange and interesting body it has. The various parts are placed next to each other, each gives a command to a certain part of the tiny ant's body and the slightest change in any of these areas would paralyze a part of its body.

The strange part is that in this small brain, which is much smaller than the head of a pin, lies a world of awareness, wisdom, civilization, taste and art. It is such that a group of scholars spend many long years of their lives, studying these animals. They include the interesting points in the books that they write for us.

Lesson 10

Can the person who created all of this awareness, wisdom, taste in such a small animals be a nature that does not itself have even a pin-head's amount of awareness and wisdom?

In the mysterious world, we know that the smallest creature recognized to date is the 'atom'. The 'atom' is so small that even the strongest microscope, one which shows a piece of straw like a mountain, is not strong enough to see one.

If you want to know how small an atom is, know that one drop of water has more atoms than the number of people upon the earth and if we want to count the protons in one centimeter of a thin wire and we get 1000 people to help us and if in each second, we separate out one of them, it will take 30 to 300 years (depending on the number of atoms) of working day and night to count all of them.

Now that you have understood that one centimeter of a thin wire contains so many atoms, just think about how many atoms are in the heavens and on the earth; in water and the air and the stars and planets and the galaxy!!

Does one's mind not tire just thinking about it? No one other than their Creator is worthy to count them.

Atoms Give us a Lesson in Monotheism

Learning about atoms, which are among the most important scientific discussions today, this tiny thing gives us a glad and happy lesson in monotheism because the world of atoms call our attention to them in four areas.

1. The extraordinary sense of order. To date, more than 100 elements have been discovered beginning gradually with one electron and accepting up to over 100; this amazing order could never be born from an unaware or unintelligent factor.

2. Strong sense of balance. We know that two different electrons attract each other. Thus electrons which are negative and a nucleus which is positive should attract each other.

In addition, we also know that the encirclement of electrons around a nucleus brings a repulsive force into being (flight from the center). Thus the pull of this force draws electrons away from the atomic environment. The atom is separated and its attractive forces want to attract the electrons and destroy the atom.

It is here that one must see how accurately the force of 'attraction' and 'repulsion' have been systematically arranged in atoms so that neither do the electrons flee nor are they attracted, but are always in a state of balance, continuing their movement. It is possible that a blind and deaf nature bring this balance into being?

3. Each upon its own way: We have said that some atoms have a multiple number of electrons but not that all of the electrons move in one circuit, but rather, in multiple circuits and each electron in a determined distance, each within its own area, with great speed move like this for millions of years, without any contradiction arising between them.

It is a simple issue to place all of these in a fixed circuit and movement with an unbelievable system of order?

4. The great energy of the atom: In order to understand the great strength of the atom, just consider that in 1945, an experimental atom bomb was set off in the wilderness. A very small atomic bomb was placed upon a metal stand. After the explosion, the metal melted and then set off steam and electricity and a frightful sound was heard. When scientists went to look for it, there was no sign of it.

In this same year, two small bombs like these were inhumanely exploded over Japan by the USA, one in the city of Nagasaki and the other in the city of Hiroshima. In the first city, 70,000 people were killed instantly and the same number were injured and in the second city, 30 to 40, 000 people were killed instantly and the same number were injured, making Japan unconditionally surrender the war with America.

Is it not sufficient to simply study the small atom for the human being to come to know the greatness of the Creator of the universe? It can then be said that there are as many reasons for the existence of God as there are atoms in the universe.

> *"And if all the trees on earth were pens and the ocean (were ink), with seven oceans behind it to add to its (supply) yet would not the words of god be exhausted"* ...
> (31:27)

Think and Answer

1. Do you know other things about the life of ants?

2. Can you draw the structure of an atom on the black board?

Appendix to Lesson Ten: How Splendid Are God's Qualities

His Qualities

Know that to the same extent that realizing the existence of God through studying the secrets of the created world is easy, learning of His Qualities is difficult and requires a great deal of care and caution.

You probably wonder why. The reason for this is clear because God does not resemble anything we have ever seen or heard. Thus the first condition to recognize God's Qualities is to negate all of the qualities of creatures, that is, not comparing Him to any limited creature of the world of nature.

It is here that our task becomes difficult because we have grown up in the heart of this nature. Our contact has been with nature. We have become familiar with it. Thus we are inclined to compare everything with it.

In other words, whatever we have seen has had a material form. Some of the creatures which have a determined time and place, have a special dimension and form. Because of this, conceiving of a God Who neither has eyes, nor time, nor place, but, at the same time, He overlooks all times and all places and is unlimited from all points of view, is a difficult task. That is, it requires that steps be taken along this way with great care.

But it is necessary to remind ourselves here of this point that we can never come to know God's Essence and we should not expect that we could because such an expectation is like expecting to contain the endless seas in a glass or expect that a child, which is developing in its mother's womb, know about all of the world outside of the womb. Is this possible?

It is here that such a small blunder will cause a person to fall tens of kilometers from the main way of coming to know God and become waylaid in crags of idol worship and the worship of creatures. Note with care that, in summary, we must be conscious of never comparing God's Qualities with the qualities of creatures.

The Qualities of Majesty and Beauty
We most often divide God's Qualities into two groups: those Qualities which God has and those Qualities which God is free from. And now, this question arises as to how many Qualities God's Essence has.

The answer is: On one hand, God's Qualities are endless and unlimited and, on the other hand, they can be summarized in one Quality because all of the Qualities of God can be summarized in the following:

The Essence of God is an essence which is infinite from all points of view and it contains all perfections.

From the point of view of Qualities which God does not contain, they can be summarized in the following sentence. The Essence of God is not imperfect from any point of view.

But from another angle, as perfections and imperfections have various levels, that is, we can conceive of endless perfections and endless imperfections, thus, it can be said that God is the infinite of demonstrated Qualities and infinite negation of Qualities because whatever perfection you can imagine, He has and whatever imperfection you can imagine, He is free of. Thus the demonstrated and negation of Qualities of God are unlimited.

The Most Well-Known Qualities of God

The most famous demonstrated Qualities of God can be summarized in the following:

1. God is the 'Knower' ('Alim): He knows all things.

2. God is Powerful (Qadir): He has ability over all things.

3. God is the Living because something which is living has wisdom, power and because God is Wise and Powerful, thus He is Living.

4. God is the Willer (Mur'id), that is, He has a Will power and He is not obliged in His work and whatever He does, has a goal and wisdom and even the smallest thing in the universe does not lack a philosophy and a goal.

5. God is Perceiving (Mudrek), that is, He understands and perceives all things. He sees everything; he hears all things and He is aware of all things.

6. God is Primordial and Eternal (Qadim and Azali), that is, He always was and His existence has no beginning because He always boils from His inner Essence and because of this, He is primordial and

eternal because a person whose being is from he himself has no non-existence or annihilation.

7. God is the Speaker (Mutakalim), that is, he can create waves in the atmosphere and speak to his Prophet, not that God has a tongue or lips or a larynx.

8. God is Truthful (Sadiq), that is, whatever He says is the Truth and is equivalent to reality because lying comes from ignorance or from weakness and a lack of Power and it is impossible for God Who is Knowing and Powerful, to lie.

The most well-known negation of Qualities of God

1. He is not a composite. That is, He does not have mixed elements because in this case, He would be in need of other elements, whereas, He is in need of nothing.

2. God is not a body because everybody is limited, unstable and accepts annihilation.

3. God is not visible. That is, He cannot be seen because if He could be seen, He would be a body, limited and accepting annihilation.

4. God has no place because He is not a body to require a place.

5. God has no partner because if He had a partner, He would have to be a limited creature because two non limited, from every point of view, is not possible and in addition, the unity of law of this world shows His Oneness.

6. His Qualities are exactly like His Essence.

7. God is Needless and Self-sufficient. He is rich and containing everything because an endless being from the point of view of knowledge, power and all things has no deficiencies.

The Holy Qur'an says:

> "There is nothing like unto Him." (42:11)

Think and Answer

1. Do you know another reason for the Oneness of God and His not having a partner?

2. Have you heard that some religions believe that God is three and some believe that He is two? Which religions are these?

Lesson 11: What is Justice?

Why was Justice selected among all of God"s Qualities, considered to be a principle of religion?

In this study, before anything else, this point must be made clear as to why the great 'ulama consider justice, one of God's Qualities, to be a principle among the five pillars of religion.

God is the Knower (*Alim*), Powerful (*Qadir*), Just (*Adil*), Wise (*Hakim*), Merciful (*Rahman*), Compassionate (*Rahim*), Primordial (*Azali*), Eternal (*Abadi*), Creator (*Khaliq*) and Sustainer (*Razzaq*). Why was only justice selected from among all of these and it became one of the five pillars of religion?

In response to this important question, several points should be noted:

1. Among God's Qualities, justice is so important that many other Qualities return to it because justice in the general, extensive sense means 'putting everything in its place'. Here, then, Hakim, Razzaq, Rahman and Rahim, and similar Qualities, are all dependent upon it.

2. Resurrection — just as we have mentioned — is related to Divine Justice as well as the mission of the Prophet and the responsibility of the Imams.

3. At the beginning of Islam, a difference of Opinion arose over the issue of the justice of the Creator:

A group of the Sunni Muslims, who were called the Ash'arites, completely denied God's justice. They said that justice and oppression make no sense in relation to God. He is the Ruler of the entire created universe. It belongs to Him and whatever He does is just.

They did not even believe in the intellect's good and evil. They said, "Our intellect alone cannot distinguish between good and bad, even the goodness of doing good or the evil of oppression..." and many such similar errors.

Another group of the Sunnis, who were called the Mu'tazilites, and all of the Shi'ites, believe in the principle of justice in relation to the Creator and they believe that God never commits oppression.

In order to separate out those two groups from one another, they called the second group, the Adliyah, in which justice (adl), as a principle, was the sign of the school and the first group were called 'qhayr adliyah' (other than justice). Shi'ites were among the 'Adliyah.

The Shi'ites, in order to distinguish their school from that of the other Adliyah, placed imamate as one of the principles as well. Thus, wherever there is a discussion of 'justice' and 'imamate', this is in reference to the Shi'ite Imami school.

As the fundamentals of religion are continuous rays of the principles of religion and as the ray of justice of the Creator is extremely effective in human society, and the most important base for human society is formed by 'social justice', the selection or choice of the principle of justice as one of the principles of religion is a means to establish justice in human society and to struggle against any kind of oppression.

Just as the unity of Essence, Qualities of the Creator, the unity of worship of Him, the light and unity of His Oneness, a solidification of human society and the unity of Qualities are strengthened, the leadership of the prophets and imams is also inspired by the issue of 'real leadership' in human society. Thus, this principle of justice of the Creator, Who rules over the entire world, is the sign of the necessity for justice in all areas of human society.

The great created universe is based upon Divine Justice. Human society will also not remain without it.

What is Justice?

Justice contains two varying meanings.

1. The extensive meaning of this word, just as we have said, is 'to put everything in its place'. In other words, it is being in balance and equilibrium. This meaning or sense of justice rules over the entire created universe, in the galaxies, within an atom, in the structure of a human being's existence and all plants and animals. This is what the famous Tradition of the Holy Prophet refers to when he says, "It is by means of justice that all of the heavens and the earth exist." For example, if the powers of 'attraction' and 'repulsion' of the earth lose their sense of balance and one of these two is removed or destroyed, the earth will be drawn towards the sun, set on fire and destroyed or it will leave its circuit and wander in the endless space of the universe until it is destroyed.

2. It is clear that the second meaning is a 'particular' one and the first one is 'general'. It should be noted that both meanings are truthful in relation to God, even though the second meaning will be more emphasized here.

The meaning of God's justice is not to remove the rights of a person nor give the rights of one to another nor to discriminate between people. He is

Lesson 11

Just in all sense of the word and the reasons or proof of His Justice will be mentioned in the next lesson.

Oppression, whether it be the taking away of a person's rights or by giving the rights of one to another, or wastage and discrimination, does not exist in the pure Essence of God. He never punishes a person who does good deeds. He never encourages a person who does evil, no one will be held responsible for the sins of another. He does not burn the wet and dry together.

Even if everyone is in error in a large society, other than one person, God separates the accounts of that one person from that of others and does not punish that person along with sinners.

And the fact that the Ash'arites said, "Even if God sends all of the prophets to hell and all of the criminals and sinners to heaven, it is not oppression,' is vain babble and baseless.

The intellect, which is never polluted with superstition and discrimination, will not listen to these ugly words.

The Difference Between Justice and Equality

Another important point which should be pointed out in this lesson is that sometimes 'justice' is confused with 'equality' and it seems that the meaning of justice is that 'equality should be maintained' whereas this is not so.

Equality is not a condition for justice. Rather, rights and priorities must be considered.

As an example, justice in a classroom of students is not that they all receive equal grades and justice between two workers is not that they receive equal wages. Rather, justice is in this that each student to be graded according to his knowledge and ability and each worker to be judged according to his work and activity.

In the world of nature, also, justice in the extensive sense means just this. If the heart of a whale, which weighs one ton, be compared to the heart of a sparrow, which is perhaps not more than one gram in weight, if they were equal, there would be no justice and if the roots of a very tall tree were equal to the roots of a small plant, this is not justice and is equivalent to oppression.

Lesson 11

Justice is that every creature receives its rights in proportion to its abilities.

Think and Answer

1. Why, among all of the Qualities of God, is Justice known to be or recognized as being one of the principles of religion?

2. Who were the Ash'arites? What do you know about their beliefs?

3. What reactions does belief in Divine Justice have in human society?

4. How many meanings does justice have? Explain them.

5. Does justice mean the same as equality?

Lesson 12: Proof or Reason for The Creator's Justice

Goodness and Evil

We have learned and it seems that this issue is necessary that our intellect distinguishes between good and evil to a certain extent. (This is that very thing which scholars speak about in ethical terms as 'goodness' and 'evil').

For instance, we know that justice and goodness are good and oppression and stinginess are evil. Before religion even mentions these things, it was clear to us. However, there are other issues which exist which our intelligence is not sufficient to understand and we must seek guidance from Divine leaders and the prophets.

Thus, if a group of Muslims in the name of the Asharites deny intellectual goodness and, evil and the way of distinguishing between 'good' and 'evil', to think that only religion brought the issue of justice and oppression, and things like this, is completely wrong.

Because if our intellect does not have the ability to choose between good and evil, how should we know whether or not God would send His message through false prophets? But the moment we say that lying is wrong and evil, and that it is impossible that

God would lie, we know that God's Promises are always true and that He is always truthful, we would never encourage deceit and never give miracles into the hands of a deceitful person.

It is here that we can rely upon what religion and the divine Law says.

Thus, we can conclude that the belief in intellectual good and evil is from religion. (Note this with care).

Now, let us return to the proof of Divine Justice. In order to understand this, we must know what is the source of oppression.

Source of Oppression

The source of oppression is one of the following things:

1. Ignorance: It sometimes happens that an oppressive person does not, in truth, know what he is doing. He does not know that he is destroying someone's rights and he is not aware of what he is doing.

2. Need: Sometimes a person is tempted to undertake a satanic act in order to attain something that another has whereas if he were self-sufficient, in

such a situation, he would have no need to commit oppression.

3. Inability: Sometimes a person is not willing to have the rights of another curtailed but he does not have the power or ability to do anything about it, and without willingness, he commits oppression.

4. Selfishness, bearing grudges and seeking revenge:

Sometimes none of these qualities exist but selfishness causes one to aggress against others or the sense of seeking revenge or bearing a grudge makes that person commit oppression or the spirit of 'exclusiveness' and 'monopolization' causes injustice to others.

But noting that none of these ugly qualities and deficiencies exist in God, because He is the Knower of all things, needless of all things, has Power over all things and is kind to all, it makes no sense for Him to commit oppression. He is a Being Who is Endless, Perfect and Unlimited.

Only Goodness, Justice and Mercy can stem from such a Being.

If He punishes those who commit evil, in reality, it is the result of their deeds which causes this, just like a person who, as a result of the use of narcotics or alcohol, is afflicted with an incurable disease. The Holy Qur'an says:

"You receive but the recompense of what you have earned." (10:52)

The Holy Qur'an and the Justice of the Creator

It is important to note that the Holy Qur'an greatly emphasizes this point:

"Verily God will not deal unjustly with man in aught. it is man that wrongs his own soul." (10:44)

And in another place, it says:

"God is never unjust in the least degree." (4:40)

"We shall set up scales of justice for the Day of Judgment so that not a soul will be dealt with unjustly in the least." (21:47)

Thus, note that what is meant by 'balance' here, is the method of weighing good and evil, not like scales of this world.

Invitation to Justice and Equity

We have said that the qualities of the human being must be like a ray of God's Qualities and in human society, God's Qualities are widespread. According to this principle, to the same extent that the Holy Qur'an stresses the Justice of the Creator, He has also stressed justice and equity in human society and the individuality of individuals.

The Holy Qur'an says that oppression and injustice will destroy society and that the fate of oppressors is of the most painful kind.

The Holy Qur'an, in addition to mentioning the fate of past tribes, has often repeated this truth for people to see the result of oppression and corruption and what punishment will be given, fear that you not suffer such a fate.

The Holy Qur'an clearly states as a principle:

"God commands justice, the doing of good and liberality to family members and He forbids all shameful deeds and injustice and rebellion..." (16:90)

It should be noted that committing oppression is an ugly act, to accept oppression and suffer suppression is also wrong according to Islam and the Holy Qur'an,

Lesson 12

"Deal not unjustly and you shall not be dealt with unjustly." (2:279)

In general, submission to inequity encourages oppression, increases suppression and aids oppressors.

Think and Answer

1. Can our intellect, independent of the Divine Law distinguish between good and evil?

2. What does oppression stem from? What is the intellectual proof of Gods Justice?

3. What does the Holy Qur'an say about the justice of the Creator and how does it negate oppression from Him?

4. What is a human being's responsibility in regard to justice and oppression?

5. Is it also a sin to submit to oppression?

Lesson 13: The Philosophy of Signs and Evil

From the earliest times to the present, a group of the unaware went against God's Justice and expressed ideas that either God's Justice did not exist or even sometimes they not only negated justice but used it as a means of proving the non-existence of God like unexpected catastrophes such as hurricanes, earthquakes, and other natural calamities, and differences of these types which can be found among people and also calamities and evil which extend to human beings or plants and animals.

Relative Judgment and Limited Knowledge

Normally, all of us, in our judgments and determination of confirmations, stress the relation things have with us. For instance, we say, such and such is near us or far from us - in other words, in relation to us.

Or such and such a person is strong or weak, that is, in comparison to our physical ability or spiritual situation.

In issues relating to good and evil and calamities and natural catastrophes, people's judgment is usually the same.

Lesson 13

For instance, if rain falls in a region, we have nothing to do with what the total effects of the rain were. We only think about our own environment, home or pasture areas, or, at the most, our own city. If it was a positive event, we say that it was God's Blessing and if negative, we call it a negative event.

When they destroy a building in order to build a new one, and we only share in its dust, we say that it was a bad event even if in the future a hospital will be built there which everyone can make use of and even if the rain had positive effects in other parts of the city.

In our normal judgments, we consider a snake bite to be a calamity without recognizing the fact that this very bite and poison is effective means of defense for this animal and disregarding the fact that sometimes from this very poison, a life-giving medicine is produced which saves the lives of thousands of people.

Thus, if we do not want to be misled, we must look at our own limitations and in our judgments, not only look at things in relation to ourselves but rather consider all sides of the issue and judge from all points of view.

In principles, events in the world are all linked together like a chain. The hurricane which hits our city today and a heavy downpour of rain which brings floods is one of these long links which is completely related to other links and is related also with an event which took place in the past and will take place in the future.

The conclusion or result is that putting one's fingers on only a small part of an issue and judging it accordingly is not to have used one's intellect and logic.

That which is worthy of creation (that which creation deserves) is complete goodness but if something, from one point of view, is evil, goodness prevails. A surgical operation is discomforting, from one point of view, and, from another, beneficial. Thus, goodness is relative.

For further development and discussion, let us look at the occurrence of an earthquake. It is true that in one area, destruction occurs but if we consider its relation to other issues, we can change our opinion.

Does an earthquake relate to the temperatures and pressure within the earth or does it relate to the attractions of the moon which continuously draw the earth towards itself and it sometimes breaks or

Lesson 13

does it relate to both? Scientists have differing views.

But whatever of these exists, the effects upon another thing must be considered. That is, we must know what effect the temperature inside the earth has in creating oil resources, which is the most important energy material in our age and also the creation of coal, etc. Thus, goodness is relative.

And also what effect the ebb and flow of the tides stemming from the pull of the moon on the oceans has upon life within the water and its creatures and often, watering a dry coast line in places where sweat water meets the oceans. This is also a relative good.

It is here that we understand what relative judgments and limited information we have when we look at issues like this as dark points which the attractions of the created world contains and however much more we look at the relationship between phenomena, we become more aware of its importance.

The Holy Qur'an tells us:

"Of knowledge, it is only a little that is communicated to you." (17:85)

Undesirable Events and Warnings

We have all seen people who when drowned in blessings, fall under the influence of price and selfishness and in this state or condition, many of the important human issues and duties are forgotten.

And, also, we have all seen that at the time of the calmness of the oceans of life and complete restfulness how such a state of sleep and forgetfulness is given a person, which, if it continues, will bring great misfortune to that person.

Without doubt, some of the undesirable events of life are in order to end that state of pride and to do away with this sleep and forgetfulness of life.

You have most certainly heard that experienced drivers complain about roads which are flat, level and lacking any twists or turns, ups or downs and they describe these attractive qualities as dangerous ones. Why?

Because the monotony of this road causes a driver to fall asleep and it is here that danger comes to him.

It has even been seen that some countries have created artificial ups and downs and put holes to prevent such a danger.

The path or way of life of a human being is also the same. If life does not have any ups or downs or potholes, and if undesirable events never occur, a state of forgetfulness of God and sleep will come and prevent a person from undertaking his or her duties and responsibilities.

We are not intimating that a human being must create undesirable events for himself or herself or welcome misfortune because calamities have continuously been and will continue to be.

Rather, we say that one must be attentive to a part of this philosophy which is to prevent pride and forgetfulness because these are enemies and barriers to well-being and happiness.

We repeat, this is the philosophy of a part of these undesirable events, not all of them because they have other aspects, as well, which, with the Will of God, will be mentioned in further lessons.

The Holy Qur'an tells us:

"When the suffering reached them from Us, why then did they not learn humility?"(6:42)

Think and Answer

1. What people have mentioned the issue of calamities and catastrophes in their ideology?

2. Mention some calamities and catastrophes. In your own life, have you ever met up with them?

3. What is meant by relative judging and total judgment and absolute evil and relative good?

4. Are earthquakes and hurricanes only harmful?

5. What positive effects can undesirable events have upon one's psyche?

Lesson 14: The Philosophy of Undesirable Events in Life

We have said that a group of the materialists have coercively made use of the issue of unpredictable occurrences of calamities and difficulties which occur in the life of human beings as an excuse to deny the justice of the Creator and sometimes, to deny even the existence of God!

Now we will continue the discussion of the previous lesson.

A Human Being is nurtured through Facing Difficulties

We again repeat that we should not create difficulties for ourselves, but, at the same time, it often happens that difficulties increase our will-power just like iron which is strengthened when placed in hot smelting pots. In the smelting pot of difficulties we become experienced and more persevering.

War is basically not good but sometimes a difficult and long war causes the abilities of a nation to blossom and transforms dispersion into unity and quickly makes up for our falling behind.

A famous Arab historian says, "The blossoming of civilization has appeared throughout history in various parts of the world. It followed a country being attacked by a powerful foreign country, being awakened and mobilizing their forces."

Of course, reactions to difficulties are not similar among all people and all societies. One group falls into despair, weakness and pessimism and reaches a negative conclusion but there are individuals who have the right attitude when faced by these difficulties and are stimulated, mobilized by them, begin to move and they are filled with excitement and enthusiasm.

But because in such situations, many people judge by what appears on the surface, they only see the bitterness and difficulties and ignore the positive and constructive effects.

We do not claim that all bitter events have such effects in a human being but at least some people are in this way.

If you study the life of geniuses of the world, you will see that almost all of them suffered difficulties and great misfortunes. There are fewer people who are raised in comfort and luxury who have shown themselves to be geniuses and who have arisen to a high position.

A good commander of an army is a person who has seen a difficult and long battle. Their economic genius' are people who have fallen into difficulties in the economic market.

Great politicians are those who have passed through hard and difficult political struggles.

In summary, we can say that the difficulties and anguishes which human beings bear, nurtures them.

The Holy Qur'an says:

"It may be that you dislike a thing and God brings about through it a great deal of good".(4:19)

Difficulties cause one to turn back to God

In the previous discussions, we have seen that, little by little, our being has a goal or purpose. Our eyes are for a purpose; our ears are for a purpose; our heart, brain and nerves each have been created for a purpose. Even our finger tips have a philosophy behind them. Thus, how is it possible that our total being be without a purpose?

At the same time, for the completion of this task, one must look every once in a while at one's sins and one's transgressions must be shown or pointed out. In facing difficulties in following God's Commands, one becomes familiar with one's ugly and evil deeds and will turn back to God. It is here that a part of the difficulties and unforeseen events are, in reality, Divine blessings.

The Holy Qur'an says:

"Corruption has appeared on land and sea because of (the deed) that the hands of men have earned, that (God) may give them a taste of some of their deeds: in order that they may turn back (from evil)." (30:41)

Noting what we have said above, painful events are confirmations of evil and interpreting them as calamities that are considered to be in opposition to Divine Justice is far from logic and intellectual reasoning because the further we go into this narrow way, we will better understand the various philosophies.

Think and Answer

1. What is the purpose of our Creation? How can we reach there?

2. How is a person strengthened by facing difficulties?

Lesson 14

3. Have you ever seen people or read about them in history who have suffered difficulties and developed themselves? Write about their Lives,

4. What does the Qur'an say in relation to our Sins?

5. Which people attain positive results from bitter events and which ones, negative results?

Lesson 15: Once Again the Philosophy of Signs and Catastrophes

Because of the fact that a discussion about signs, catastrophes, sudden events and unpleasant events is a very difficult and complicated one and is most often discussed in the area of ontology and monotheism we are obligated to the student to study this issue further from another point of view which is more readily understandable by the general reader.

Difficulties and Ups and Downs give Spirit to Life

Perhaps it is difficult for some people to understand that if life was only filled with blessings, it would lose its value.

It has been proven today that if you place an object in the middle of a room, and you give it a strong, uniform light from all directions and the object and the room both be completely smooth, we will not be able to see the object because when shadows are placed next to light, the dimension of the form is made clear and the shadow separates the object from the light and then we can see it.

The value of the gifts of life as well as the weak or strong shadows of difficulties cannot be seen. If throughout life, there were no such thing as sickness; the pleasure of health would never be sensed. Following a night of a high fever and the morning dawn, when the fever breaks, the memory of such a night, when one regains one's health and thinks back on that night of fever and pain, one realizes what a jewel good health is.

In general, a uniform kind of life, even the most comfortable kind of life is tiresome, spiritless and death like. It has often been seen that individuals, because of a comfortable life, empty of any kind of difficulties, find it so boring that they attempt to commit suicide or else they continuously complain about their life.

You will find no architect with taste who will design the walls of a large room to be totally smooth and uniform. Rather, he carves curves and lines into it.

Why is the world of nature so beautiful? Why is the view of jungles which fill the sides of mountains and streams with twists and turns among the small and large trees so interesting and attractive?

One reason is the lack of uniformity.

The order of light and darkness and the coming and going of day and night which the Holy Qur'an emphasizes in various verses, has a great effect upon ending any kind of a tiresome life of human beings, why?

Because if the sun continuously be in one place in the sky and uniformly give light to the earth, if its position never changed and night would never come, in addition to the other problems this would have, in a short period of time, all human beings would get tired.

It is because of this that we must accept that at least most of the problems caused by unforeseen events give a spirit to life, making it sweet and bearable. It manifests the values of blessings and gives the human being the possibility to benefit from the gifts to the extent possible.

Difficulties one makes for one's self

Another point which we feel it is necessary to mention at the end of this discussion is that many people fall into error in their reckoning of the causes and effects of unforeseen events and the oppression which takes place through the hands of oppressors are considered to be signs of the injustice of the Creator of the world and the disorder in the work of humanity is considered to be the fault of disorder in the structure of creation.

Just as they sometimes say, "Why is each stone made to block the way?" Why do some earthquakes strike cities and cause little damage but in the rural areas, many people are taken as sacrifices and many lose their lives in the fallen refuge of their homes. What kind of justice is this?

If calamity is to be divided, why is it not divided up equally?

Why the edge of sorrowful catastrophes always falls upon the deprived people?

Why in contagious diseases, these people most often suffer?

These are all beside the fact and do not relate to the system of creation and justice of God. These are the results of oppression, exploitation and colonialism of human beings in relation to one another.

If it were not for the fact that the rural people are abased and poverty-stricken because of the oppression of the cities and they were able to build better and stronger homes for themselves like those in the cities, earthquakes would not have such an effect upon them.

But when their houses are built of mud or stones or wood and very little stucco or cement is used in the building of their homes, and in a simple way, it is piled on top of each other, even a strong wind or a very slight earthquake makes the earth open up, we should not expect the situation to be better than this. But what does this have to do with God?

This criticism should be made against the unbalanced situation and erroneous system of society. We must arise and end these injustices to society. We must fight with abasement and poverty and give the deprived their rights so that such phenomena do not appear.

If all groups of society have sufficient nourishment health and treatment, they will be able to face diseases and sicknesses with greater strength and perseverance.

But when an erroneous and false social system rules a society in the form of colonialism, one person is given so many possibilities that even their cats and dogs have a doctor, medicine and receive special medical care, but others do not have even the most basic necessities of life and health to care for their children, such unpleasant scenes are plentiful and are seen by all.

Instead of complaining about God in such situations, we should reproach ourselves.

We have to tell oppression not to be oppressive! And we have to tell the oppressed not to bear oppression!

We must make efforts so that all individuals of a society have at least the minimum amount of health facilities, food and housing, educational and cultural possibilities.

In summary, we should not place the blame for our sins on Creation. When did God ever impose a system like this upon us? Where has He ever recommended this?

Of course, He created us free because our being free is the key to our development and progress. But it is we who misuse our freedom and oppress each other and this oppression then shows itself as unevenness in society. But unfortunately, this error has come to include a great many people.

The Holy Qur'an says:

"Verily God will not deal unjustly with man in aught: it is man that wrongs his own soul." (10:44)

And now we end the discussion of signs and catastrophes here even though there is still a great deal which could be said, but this brief discussion is sufficient for us in this short study.

Think and Answer

1. Why did the discussion on signs and catastrophes continue for three lessons?

2. What ill effects does a uniform and monotonous life have? Have you ever seen a person who has a high life style, suffer?

3. What can we surmise from the light and darkness in the world of creation?

4. Do all of the difficulties which exist in society relate to Creation or are we also responsible?

5. To do away with social inequalities, does a correct way exist? What duty do we have towards the deprived?

Lesson 16: The Issue of Predestination & Free Will

One of the issues which is directly related to the issue of the justice of the Creator, is the question of predestination or free will.

According to the fatalists (those who believe in predestination), a human being has no choice whatever in his or her acts, behavior or words and the movements of his organs are just like the predestined movements of tile parts of a machine.

Thus, this question arises, how does this opinion relate to Divine Justice? And perhaps because of this, the group of the Asharites — the group we previously mentioned, who deny intellectual good and evil — have accepted predestination and deny justice. Why? Because when one accepts predestination, justice makes no sense.

In order to further clarify this point, we are obliged to study several subjects with care:

The Roots of the Belief in Predestination

All people within their being sense that they are free to make decisions. For example, whether or not to give a loan to such and such a friend or that one drinks a glass of water placed before one, if one so desires or does not drink it or if another person commits an error in relation to this person, this second person can forgive or not forgive the error or that everyone distinguishes a hand which shakes because of illness or old age from a hand which one purposefully causes to shake.

In spite of the fact that the issue of free will is a general human sense, why do some people follow the school of the fatalists?

Of course, there are several important reasons which we shall recall here and they are that a human being sees that an environment has an effect upon another person, education is another, propaganda and social culture also, without doubt, affect the thoughts and spirit of a person.

Sometimes, even, one's economic position can provide a motive for movement in a human being and one cannot deny a factor.

The totality of these cause one to assume that a person does not have free will, but rather that the external and internal factors join hands and force us to make a decision and that if these factors did not exist, we would not be faced with these problems.

These are things which can be called 'the environmental determinants', 'economic determinants', 'educational determinants' and predestination are among the factors considered to be important by the school of fatalists.

The Main Error of the Fatalists

But those who think this way have forgotten an important point and it is that the discussion is not about motives and defective causes; the discussion is about complete causes.

In other words, no one can deny the role played by the environment, culture and economics in the thoughts and acts of a human being. The discussion is that with all of these motives, the final decision still remains with us.

Because we clearly sense that even in an erroneous system, one which rebels against God's Commands like the monarchial system of the past, which had laid the groundwork for deviation, we were not obliged to deviate and to go to the centers of corruption.

Thus, one must distinguish between and separate out bases and complete causes. Because of this, a great many people who live in comfort or have been nurtured in a deviated culture or they inherited unsuitability, at any rate, have separated their way from that of others, and have either arisen or revolted against that environment, if every human being was supposed to be the child of his or her environment, culture and propagation of the times, no real or basic revolution would ever take place in the world, every one would have to adapt to his or her environment, and never build a new one.

All of these show that the above mentioned factors do not make one's destiny, they are only bases; one's principle or main fate is determined by one's own will power.

This is exactly as if we were to decide on a very hot summer day to fast according to God's Commands, all of our body needs water while it is possible that in order to obey God, we ignore all of this whereas it is possible others follow this request and not fast. Thus, all motives which cause one's destiny exist within the human being's free will.

The Social and Political Factors of the School of Fatalism

The truth is that the issue of predestination and free will throughout history has been misused. A series of predestined factors have increased the belief in fatalism and the denial of free will of the human being. Among them:

Political Factors

Many of the despotic and selfish politicians in order to extinguish the fire of revolution among the deprived, in order to assure the continuation of their illegal rule (for every rule or regime which oppresses the people and denies people their rights is illegal from the point of view of Islam), convince the people through all the means available to them, that they have no free will, that predestination and predetermination of history holds our destiny in its hands. If one group rules and another is ruled, this is a rule of fate and destiny of history!

It is clear how this kind of thinking can narcotize people and aids the policies of colonialism whereas according to our intellect and our Divine Law, our destiny and fate lies in our own hands and fate and destiny in the sense of predestination and predetermination does not exist. Divine fate and destiny is determined through our movements, desires, will-power, faith, efforts and endeavors we make.

Psychological Factors: Laziness and Indifference

Lazy, indifferent and lethargic individuals exist who most often meet up with defeat in life and they never desire to admit this bitter truth that their laziness or errors have caused their defeat.

Thus, in order to avoid confronting themselves with the deficiencies and developing themselves into better people, they turn to fatalism and they think that their sin is a result of coercive fate so that in this way they can find a false 'sense of security'.

They say, "What can be done? We were blackened from the beginning. It. will not be whitened even with the water of Zamzam or Kawthar. We are extremely talented and make great efforts, but unfortunately, we have no luck."

Social Factors

Some people want to be free to be able to follow their carnal desires and every sin which is to their liking they want to commit and, at the same time, somehow convince themselves that they are not sinners and deceive society that they are sinless!

It is here that they turn to fatalism and their carnal desires with the justification that we have no free will to choose not to do these things. But they well know that all of these are lies and even those who make such claims and raise such issues know that they are baseless but their pleasures and passing fantasies do not allow them to admit this truth.

Thus, in order to build a healthy society, we must struggle against this fatalist way of thinking, belief in one's coercive destiny which are tools used in the hands of colonialism and exploitation and an instrument to deceitfully justify defeat and the factor which causes corruption to progress in a society.

Think and Answer

1. What is the difference between the schools of fatalism and free will?

2. What causes one to choose fatalism?

3. What answer can you give to the effects of environment, culture and heritage?

4. What are the political, psychological and social factors which cause an extension in the beliefs of fatalism?

5. What position should we take when confronted by these factors?

Lesson 17: The Clearest Reason for Free Will

The General Conscience of Human Beings Denies Predestination

Even if philosophers and divine scholars give different reasons for free will of the human being, here we will take a short cut and give the clearest reason given by the supporters of free will and this is the 'universal' or 'collective' conscience of human beings.

That is, no matter what we deny, we cannot deny this reality that in all human societies, including both the worshipers of God and the materialists, East and West, ancient and modern, wealthy and poor, developed or undeveloped, of whatever culture, all without exception, agree that a law should rule human beings and that human beings are responsible before the law and people who disobey the law must be punished.

In other words, the rule of law, the responsibility of individuals before it and the punishment of those who disobey the law are things which all intelligent people agree with and it was only savage, primitive tribes who did not officially recognize these three things.

Lesson 17

The fact that we explain this as the general conscience of human beings of the world is the clearest proof of the existence of free will in human beings and the fact that they have free choice.

How can it be accepted that a human being be obliged in his or her actions and that he or she have no freedom of choice but he or she is responsible before the law? And that when a law is broken, that person must be tried and asked why he or she did this or that or did not do this or that.

And if proven guilty, that person is sent to prison or even, depending upon the crime, executed, this is exactly as if we were to punish stones which slide down a mountain causing a landslide on a mountain road which results in the death of one or more human beings.

It is true that a human being differs from a stone, but if we deny free will and choice in a human being, this external difference between them will not be relevant and both will be the victims of fate. A stone, following the law of gravity, falls upon the roadside and a human being who murders another, is the victim of another factor of fate.

Thus, the logic of those who believe in predetermination allows for no distinction to be made between a stone and a human being from the point of view of result and neither acted according to their own free will. Why should one be tried and not the other?

We are at a crossroad. We either have to deny existence of the common conscience of all of the people of the world and consider the courts, punishment of those who disobey the law to be ridiculous and useless and even oppressive or deny the beliefs of the fatalists. Obviously the latter is preferable.

It is interesting to note that those who believe in the school of fatalism, and give reasons for their belief, when they are faced with a real life situation, they act according to free will!

For instance, if a person aggresses against them, or annoys or bothers them, they take this person to court and do not rest at ease until that person is punished.

Well, if it is really true that a person has no choice or free will, what are all of this commotion and court and trial about?

Lesson 17

At any rate, this common conscience of the intelligent of the world is a living idea for the reality that human beings have accepted the existence of free will in the depths of their being and has always been loyal to that and cannot live without the belief for even one day and have the wheels of social and individual programs progress.

A great Iranian philosopher, Khawjeh Nair al-din Tusi, in discussing predestination and free will says in one short sentence in his book Kitab Tajrubah bih al-Aqa'id, "Our necessary understanding and conscience tells us that we are responsible for all of our deeds."

The Contradiction Between the Logic of Predestination and Free Will

That which we have said above was about the contradiction between the school of predestination and the common conscience of the intelligence of the world, both from the point of view of supporters of religion and people who do not at all accept religion.

But from the point of view of religious thought, there is another sure reason for recognizing the falsity of the school of fatalism.

As religious belief can never agree with fatalism, religious programs, as well, are all altered by accepting this school of thought.

How can we reconcile the justice of God which we proved in previous lessons with the school of fatalism? How is it possible that God oblige someone to do an evil deed? Then punish him because he did it. This does not agree with any kind of logic!

Thus, by accepting the school of fatalism, spiritual rewards, punishments, heaven and hell are meaningless as well as 'scroll of deeds', 'questioning', 'Divine reckoning', 'reprimanding the evil doers in the Qur'an', 'encouragement and praise for those who do good', all of these lose their meaning. Because according to this school, neither do the good doers or the evil doers have a choice.

In addition, in religion, one of the first issues we encounter is 'duty' or 'responsibility', but does 'duty' or 'responsibility' make any sense if a person has no choice?

Can we tell a person whose hands involuntarily shake, not to shake their hands? Or tell a person who is falling down a steep mountain to standstill?

It is because of this that Imam 'Ali, peace be upon him, says in a famous tradition recorded in the Usul al-Kafi, vol. 1, p. 119, that the school of fatalism is a school of idol worship whose followers are members of Iblis' party: 'These words of idol worshipping brothers, enemies of God members of Iblis' party."

Think and Answer

1. What is the clearest reason for the falsity of fatalism?

2. Describe the general or common conscience people of the world which believes in the principle of free will.

3. Do the followers of the school of fatalism according to their beliefs?

4. Does fatalism agree with the principle of Divine justice? If not, why?

5. Why is free will the basis for accepting any kind duty or responsibility?

Lesson 18: A World of Wonder in a Small Bird: What is the 'Middle Way'?

'Conferring' as opposed to 'Fatalism'

Of course, opposing the belief in fatalism, which is one kind of an extreme, is the school of 'conferring', which is at the other extreme.

Those who accept this school believe that God created us and then put everything at our disposal and that, in general, He is not responsible for anything that we do and in this way, we are completely independent in choosing what we do.

Doubtlessly, this belief does not agree with monotheism because monotheism has taught us that God rules the entire world and nothing is beyond His control. Even our free will and free choice cannot be beyond His realm, otherwise polytheism would, of necessity, result.

In other words, we cannot believe in two gods, one, the great Creator of the universe and the other, a small one who is the human being who is free to do whatever he or she wishes, completely free and independent and even God cannot affect what he or she wishes to do.

This is duality and polytheism. What is important is that we know human beings have freedom of choice and free will at the same time that we know God to be the Ruler over all persons and deeds.

The School of the 'Middle Way'

The fine point to recognize is here, that we not imagine that there is a contradiction between the two. The fact is that we both accept God's justice as well as the freedom and responsibility of His servants as well as unity and His rule over the entire universe of existence and this is that very thing which is known as the 'middle way' (something which is between two extremes).

Let us clarify this with an example as the issue is a very complicated one. Let us assume that you are traveling on an electric train and you are the driver of the train.

A strong electric cable has been placed along the line of the train and the train is connected with a link to this electric cable and moves and moment after moment the electricity is passed to the locomotive in such a way that if for just one moment, the electricity to the locomotive stops, the whole train will stop.

Without doubt, you are free. You can stop wherever you want and you can move at your own speed. But in spite of all of this freedom, the person who is sending the electricity can, at any moment, make you stop because all of your power and strength is that very electricity and he holds the key.

When we note this example with care, we see that even though one has such freedom, choice and responsibility, one is completely at the disposal of the power of another and these two do not contradict each other.

Another example:

Assume that the hand muscles of a person as the result of illness or the occurring of an unforeseen event, do not work and he does not have the power to move his hand but if we connect that to a very small amount of electricity, the nerves will be warmed and become capable of movement.

Whenever such a person commits a crime with that hand, for instance, and in that very state, strikes another person in their face, strikes a knife in an innocent person, it is clear who the person responsible is because he both had the power and the choice and a person who has will power is responsible for what he does.

But at the same time, that person who gives his hand electricity and creates his power and strength, rules over him and while he is free and has a choice, he is in his grasp.

Now let us return to the main point.

God has given us physical power or strength and from moment to moment, it continues and if it is cut off for even a moment, and our connection with Him be cut off, we would be destroyed.

If we can do anything it is because we have strength which He has given us and it continues moment by moment and even our freedom and choice is also from Him. That is, He willed that we be free and by making use of this great Divine kindness, one can transform one's self.

Thus, at the same time that we have free choice and a free will, we are in His grasp and we will never move beyond His realm. At the same time that we have strength and power, we are dependent upon Him and without Him, we will be destroyed and this is what "the middle way' means because neither have we recognized any creature to be equal to God, which would bring multi-theism nor do we believe creatures are obliged to act as they do which would bring oppression.

We have learned this lesson from our pure Imams, peace be upon them. Whenever they were asked, "Does anything exist between fatalism and conferring?" They said, "Yea. More extensive than the distance between heaven and earth." (See *Usul al-Kafi*, vol. 1, p. 121)

The Holy Qur'an and Fatalism and Free Will

The Holy Qur'an states this issue directly and proves the free will of human beings and there are hundreds of verses which talk about free will.

1. All of the verses which relate to commanding to virtue and preventing vice are all proof of the free will of human beings because if a person was obliged to do so, doing so would make no sense.

2. All of the verses which blame and reproach the evil doers and praise the good doers are proof of free will because if one was obliged to do whatever one did, blame or praise would make no sense.

3. All of the verses which talk about the questioning on the Day of Judgment and the Judgment in that Court and then the rewards and punishments and heaven and hell are proof of free will because if one was to assume that everything was predestined then

questioning, judging, rewards and punishments would all be oppressive.

4. All of the verses which say that a human being is responsible for his or her deeds:

"Every soul will be (held) in pledge for its deeds." (74:38)

"(Yet) in each individual in pledge for his deeds." (52:21)

Verses like:

"We showed him the Way: whether he be grateful or ungrateful (rests on his will)." (76:3)

"But you will not except as God Wills..." (76:30)

Think and Answer

1. What is meant by 'conferring' and what error is hidden in it.

2. Describe, in a clear way, the 'middle way' which we learned from the Imams and give examples.

3. What does the Holy Qur'an say about free will and predestination?

4. If we accept the idea of fatalism, what happens to spiritual rewards and punishments and heaven and hell? Is the verse, "But you will not except as God Wills..." (76:30), a proof of fatalism?

Lesson 19: Guidance and Error are in God's Hands

The Parts of Guidance and Error

A traveler has an address in his hand. He meets you and asks you to help him find the address. You have two choices before you:

First, to go with him and complete your good deed by accompanying him to his destination and then say good-bye and leave him.

Second, indicate with your hand and giving various signs guide him towards his destination.

It is evident that in both cases, you have guided him towards his destination but there is a difference between these two; the second one is just expressing way and the first, is taking one to one's destination. The Holy Qur'an and Traditions of Islam mention both ways.

On the other hand, sometimes guidance only has legal quality to it, that is, formed by means of laws and rules and sometimes it has an instinctive quality, that is, by means of facilities provided by creation like the guidance of a seed to becoming a complete human being and both of these ways are mentioned in the Holy Qur'an and the Traditions.

By clarifying the means of guidance (and, naturally the point opposite it, leading astray or error), we return to the main discussion.

We read in many of the verses of the Holy Qur'an that guidance and leading astray is God's work. Doubtlessly, the 'indication of the way' comes from God. Why? Because He sent the Prophet and sent the heavenly Book to show people the way.

But 'reaching the goal' through coercion or force clearly does not agree with free will and choice but because all power and strength which is necessary to reach one's goal God gives us and it is He Who gives us success upon this way, this sense of guidance is also from God, that is, preparation of the equipment and the preliminaries and providing them is at the disposal of humanity.

An Important Question

Now, an important question arises, and that is what we read in many verses of the Holy Qur'an:

"God guides whom He wills and misleads whom He wills."
(14:4)

Some people, without considering other verses of the Holy Qur'an, and the interpretation which one verse has with others, immediately, upon seeing this verse, object and say, "If God guides whom He wills and misleads whom He wills, what are we supposed to do in the middle?"

The important point is that the verses of the Holy Qur'an must always be studied in relation to each other in order to understand them in truth. Here we will recall several other verses about guidance and leading astray so that you can study them in relation to the above verse:

"God will establish in strength those who believe, with the Word that stands firm in this world and in the hereafter; but God will leave, to stray, those who do wrong: God does what He wills." (14:27)

"Thus does God leave to stray such as transgress and live in doubt." (40:34)

"And those who strive in Our (Cause), We will certainly guide them to Our paths: for verily God is with those who do right." (29:69)

As we see, God's will is not unaccountable. He neither gives the success of guidance to a person nor does He deny a person success. Those who undertake the jihad upon God's Way, war with their difficulties and show strength and firmness of purpose, have been promised guidance and this is justice.

But those who create oppression and suppression and those who take steps towards extravagance, doubt, injustice and causing temptation in hearts, God takes away their possibility of guidance.

Their hearts, as a result of these deeds, are darkened and they will not be able to succeed in reaching the station of well-being. This is how the Creator leaves the results of our deeds in our own hands and this is justice.

Knowledge of the Eternal is a cause to Arise

The last point which we feel should be mentioned here in the discussion of predestination and free will is the excuse used by some fatalists as knowledge of the eternal of God.

They say, "Does God know that so and so at such and such an hour on such and such a day will kill someone or will drink an alcoholic beverage?" If we say, "He does not know," we have denied God's knowledge and if we say, "Yes, that person must do this, otherwise God's knowledge will be imperfect."

Lesson 19

Thus, in order to preserve God's knowledge, a person is obliged to sin and obey God!!

But the fact is, this excuse was fabricated in order to cover over the sins they wanted to commit but they have forgotten the fact that we say that God knew from eternity whether we would be inclined towards free will and choice and will obey or sin. That is, our will or choice was also part of God's knowledge. Thus, if we are obliged to sin, God's knowledge will become ignorant. (Pay careful attention here).

Allow us to put forth some questions on this point to clarify them. Assume that a teacher knows that a lazy student will fail at the end of the year and the teacher is one hundred percent sure of this fact because of years of experience as a teacher.

When the student fails, can the student take the teacher to task and say, "Your knowledge and what you foresaw caused me to fail."

Or, let us assume that he is a sinless and pure person and he knew of a murder which would take place on such and such a day and interferes to prevent it, does the knowledge of this pure person take away the responsibility of the criminal, obliging the criminal to commit the crime?

Or, assume that a new machine has been invented which can predict the occurrence of an event several hours before it happens and it can say that so and so at such and such an hour in such and such a place will commit such and such an act. Does this oblige that person to do this?

In summary, Gods knowledge never obliges anyone to do anything.

Think and Answer

1. How many kinds of guidance are there? Describe them.

2. Recite the verses of the Qur'an which describe God's guidance and leading astray.

3. What is the interpretation of God's guidance and leading astray?

4. What is meant by Gods eternal knowledge?

5. Does this knowledge withdraw our duty and responsibility? Give an example.

Lesson 20: God's Justice and the Issue of Eternity

We know that the Holy Qur'an directly speaks of the eternal punishment to be given to the *kuffar*. That is, it speaks about eternity.

> *"God has promised the hypocrites, men and women, and the kafirs, the fire of hell," therein shall they dwell," sufficient is it for them; for them is the curse of God, and an en during punishment." (9:68)*

Just as in the verse following that, the Qur'an promises the believing men and the believing women gardens in Paradise forever.

"God has promised to believers, men and women, gardens under which rivers flow, to dwell therein and beautiful mansions in gardens of everlasting bliss. But the greatest bliss is the good pleasure of God, that is, the supreme felicity." (9:72)

This question then arises and that is, how can one accept that in one's lifetime of eighty or one hundred years, one commits evil deeds and then for eternity — millions of years — is punished.

Of course, this is not important as to rewards because the ocean of God's Mercy is very great and however much greater is the reward, it shows greater virtue and mercy but as to evil deeds, they are punished for eternity because of limited sins. How can this be reconciled with God's justice? Should a balance not exist between punishment and reward?

Answer: In order to reach a final solution to this discussion, several points need to be noted:

Punishments on the Day of Resurrection do not resemble punishments in this world. For instance, a person is found guilty of aggression and plunder and he spends some time in prison whereas the punishment at the Judgment takes the form of efforts of one's deeds and the particularities of a person's acts.

In clearer terms, the difficulties which one bears in the other world are the direct result of his deeds. The Holy Qur'an explains this very clearly where it says,

"Then on that Day, not a soul will be wronged in the least and you shall but be repaid the meeds of your past deeds." (36:54)

With one simple example, we can visualize this truth that a person who goes after narcotics and alcoholic drinks and no matter how much one explains that

Lesson 20

these things will ruin him, and sicken his heart and destroy his nerves, he does not listen.

He spends several weeks or months drowned in these killing pleasures and gradually develops ulcers, heart disease, nerve disease and then he spends tens of years until the end of his life suffering because of this and he groans night and day.

Can one object here why does a person who only sinned for several weeks or months have to suffer for tens of years?

It is readily stated in response that this is the result of his own actions. Even if he were to live longer than the Prophet Noah and were to live for tens of thousands of years and we were to continuously see him in pain and anguish, we would say that this is something he brought upon himself with his deeds.

Punishment on the Day of Judgment is like this.

Thus, no one can object to the justice of the situation.This is wrong that some people assume that the time limit of the punishment must be the same extent as the sin because the relation between a sin and punishment is not a temporal one. It depends upon the result and quality of the sin.

For instance, it is possible that a person in one second kills an innocent person and according to the laws of some countries, he is given life imprisonment. Here we see that the time of the sin was one quickly passing second, whereas the punishment is for tens of years. No one considers this to be oppressive.

Why? Because the question here is not one of days or weeks or months or years. It depends upon the quality of the sin and its result. Eternity in hell and eternal punishment only belongs to those people who have closed all doors to salvation for themselves and they have drowned themselves in corruption, licentiousness, kufr and hypocrisy so that the darkness of sin takes over their entire being and, as a result, that person takes on the color of sin and kufr.

The Holy Qur'an says:

"Nay, those who seek gain in evil and are girt round by their sins — they are companions of the fire: therein shall they abide (forever)." (2:81)

These kinds of individuals have completely cut off their connection with God and have closed all doors to their salvation and well-being.

These kinds of individuals are like birds which purposefully break their own wings, pull out their feathers, are obliged to walk forever upon the earth and are deprived of flying through the skies.

Noticing the three points given above clarifies the issue that eternal punishment which belongs to a particular group of hypocrites or kufar does not oppose the principle of justice. This is the ominous result of their deeds themselves. The Divine Prophets had previously told them that their deeds would have these results.

It is clear that if individuals are ignorant and the invitation of the prophets not are known to them and if they commit evil deeds out of ignorance, they will not receive such a difficult punishment.

It is also necessary to point out that verses of the Holy Qur'an and Islamic Traditions are used because the ocean of Divine Mercy is so great and extensive that a large group of transgressors are included. Some by means of intercession; some by means of forgiveness and some because of small, good deeds which they performed. God, in His greatness, gives great reward for those small, good deeds.

And another group, after they have been punished for a time in hell, and have been purified, they will return because of Divine Mercy.

The only group remaining is the one which has enmity towards the truth and commit oppression, corruption and hypocrisy so that their whole being is covered in oppression, *kufr* and faithlessness.

Think and Answer

1. How is it that some people think that eternity does not conform to Divine Justice?

2. Are the punishments in the other world similar to the punishment in this world? If not, what are they like?

3. Does justice demand that there be a balance between the time of a sin and its punishment?

4. Who will receive eternal punishment?

5. Who will receive Divine Forgiveness?

Lesson 21: Our Need for Divine Leaders

The Limitations of Our Knowledge

There are people who might perhaps ask if sending of the prophets by God is necessary to guide the people. Is our intellect not sufficient to understand the realities? Is the progress and development of science not sufficient to discover all of the secrets and illuminate all of the truths?

And then whatever the prophets might tell us, is one of two things which either our intellect understands well or it does not.

In the first case, we do not need the prophets and as to the second, we cannot accept something which goes against our intellect and wisdom.

On the other hand, is it correct for the human being to be placed completely in the hands of others and accept whatever they say without questioning? Are the prophets not human beings just like we are? How can we agree to place ourselves at the disposal of what another human being says?

Answers: Noting the following points, the position of the Holy Prophet in the system of the life of human beings will be come clear.

We should recognize the fact that our knowledge is limited and with all of the progress which humanity has made in science and technology, still that which we know, in comparison to that which we do not know, is like a drop in comparison to an ocean.

As some of the great scientists say, all of the knowledge that we have at our disposal at the present time, can only be considered to be the abc's of the great book of the world of creation.

In other words, the realms, judgments and comprehension of our intellect are a small area which has been lit by our knowledge. In truth, our intellect is like a strong spot light but the prophets and heavenly revelation are like a sun which shines upon the earth. Can a person say, "As I have a spot light, I no longer need the sun??!!"

Even a clearer example: Life's issues can be divided into three groups, 'intelligent', 'unintelligent' and 'unknown'.

The prophets never say anything which was 'unintelligent', that is, something against the intellect or wisdom and if they do, they are not prophets, rather, they help us in the understanding of unknowns and this is very important for us.

Thus, those in the past who said that if a person has intelligence, he does not need a prophet or like those who today say that with all of the knowledge that the human being has today, there is no need for prophets and their teachings, have not understood the realms of the intelligence and knowledge of the human being, nor the mission of the prophets.

This is just like a child who has studied the abc's in the first grade and then says, "I know everything and so I have no need of a teacher." Are these not baseless words?

The prophets are not just teachers, either; the story of their leadership is something which needs to be discussed separately, which we will do in later lessons.

No one says that a human being should place themselves completely at the disposal of another person. The point is that the prophets — as we will later prove — are related to divine revelation, that is, with the endless knowledge of God, and we must, by means of certain and sure reasons, know their relation to God. It is only then that the words of these heavenly messages can be accepted and we accept their reckoned teachings with all of our hearts and being.

If I follow the prescriptions of an expert physician, have I erred? The prophets are great doctors of the spirit. If I accept the lessons of a teacher which are coordinated with the intellect, have I done something wrong? The prophets are the great teachers of humanity.

More important than this is that we carefully study the reason for the necessity of God sending the prophets to us. There are three reasons why we need the guidance of the prophets from God:

The Need of Teachings

If we ride upon a fantastic and fairy tale-like horse which is built of rays of light and in every second we travel 300,000 kilometers in the shoreless space, doubtlessly we will need to have thousands of lifetimes of Noah just to see a small part of this extensive universe.

It is clear that this universe, with its greatness, was not created uselessly and as we learned in our study of God, the creation of this world has no benefit to God's state, because He is a Being Who is totally and absolutely free from any need, Who is eternal and He has no deficiency which He could want to meet by the creation of the world and humanity.

Lesson 21

Thus, we can conclude that His goal was to give Mercy to others and to help creatures reach perfection, just like the fact that the sun shines upon us without it having any need of us. This light and heat of the sun is only to our advantage and benefit because what do we do for the sun?

On the other hand, is our intelligence and knowledge sufficient for us to move along towards the way of perfection and the reaching towards becoming a perfect human being?

What amount of the secrets of the world do we know?

What is the truth of life?

When was this world created? No one knows the answer to these questions.

How long will it remain? Again, no one knows the answer to this.

Every scholar of humanity has an opinion from the social and economic point of view.

For instance, one group recommends capitalism and another group, socialism or communism and another group, neither accepts this group nor that, and considers both to be harmful.

In other issues of life, as well, there are differences of opinions among the scholars.

A human being falls into a state of wonder as to which one of all of these to accept.

It is here that, in all fairness, we must admit that in order to reach the main goal of creation, that is, perfection and nourishment of the human being in all areas, we need a series of teachings which are correct and empty of any error; ones which rely upon the realities of life, teachings which can help us, upon this long road, to reach the main goal.

This can only be done through God's knowledge, that is, divine revelation through the prophets. Because of this, God Who created us to take this journey, must place the knowledge at our disposal.

The Need for Leadership in the Social and Moral Areas

We know that within our being, in addition to knowledge and wisdom, other motives called 'instincts' also exist, the instinct of self-love, the instinct of anger and harshness, the instinct of lust and multiple other instincts.

Without doubt, if we do not control our instincts, and they dominate over us, even our knowledge and intellect will be imprisoned, and the human being, like the oppressors of history, will be changed into wolves which are far more dangerous than the wolf of the wilderness.

We need a teacher to learn ethics. We need a model so that we can learn from him according to the principle whereby one narrates something and others follow.

A perfect and disciplined human being, from every point of view, is required to take our hand upon this way, which is full of twists and turns, and prevent the rebellion of our instincts, to have virtuous .principles and his deeds and words sit upon our hearts and very beings, nurture courage, bravery, friendship with other human beings, brotherhood, forgiveness, loyalty, correctness, trustworthiness and purity within our spirits.

What person, other than a pure and immaculate prophet, could be chosen to be such a teacher and guide?

For this very reason, it is not possible that God not show His Mercy to us and prevent us from the existence of such leaders and teachers. (A discussion on this will continue in the next lesson).

Think and Answer

1. Do you feel that with whatever knowledge you gain, what you do not know has increased? (Give examples)

2. Can you clarify the difference between blind imitation and being followers of the prophets?

3. If, without a guide, we take the unknown road, what dangers will exist for us?

4. Describe the dimension of our need for leader ship of the prophets.

5. Can you guess what other discussion remains in this area to complete this discussion

Lesson 22: The Need of having Prophets who Present The Law

In the previous lesson, we came to know the need for the existence of the prophets from the two dimensions of learning and training. Now we have reached the point where we need to know the social laws and the important role of the prophets in this area.

We know that the greatest privilege of life for the human being, which is the factor for all of the progress in all of the various areas of life, is a dynamic social encounter.

Most certainly, if human beings lived apart from each other, they would still be like the human beings in the Stone Age from the point of view of knowledge and civilization.

Yes. It is the united efforts and endeavors which light the lamp of culture and civilization. It is united efforts and endeavors which are the source and origin for all of these scientific discoveries.

As an example, if we consider the journey to the moon, we see that this was not the result of the work of one or several scientists. Rather, it has been the result of the efforts of millions of scholars over thousands of years and the experiences of scholars gained through group living and then this knowledge reached the point where we find it today.

If a skilled physician in our age succeeds to transplant the living heart of a human being from the body of a dead person into the body of another person and save him from certain death, this has been made possible from the results of the experiences of thousands of physicians and surgeons throughout history which, by means of teachers, has been transferred to their students.

But, of course, social life, on the other hand, does present difficulties in the conflicts which arise between the rights and interests of human beings with each other, resulting sometimes in aggression and even war.

It is here that the need exists for law, programming and clear rules? Laws can solve three great problems for us.

1. Laws define the duties of each individual in relation to society. Social duties are clarified and talents are coordinated which blossom among human beings.

2. Laws coordinate the methods to be used to carry out one's responsibility by every individual.

3. Laws prevent the aggression of individuals against the rights of each other; they prevent chaos and conflicts between individuals and groups and, when necessary, punishments are provided for aggressors.

Who is the best lawgiver?

Now we have to see what person is best to bring laws which meet the human being's needs in such a way that all three principles mentioned above are followed and included as well as clarifying the limits, duties and rights of the individual and society so that the best system be put to use and aggression be prevented.

Let us to give a simple example here.

Human society can be compared to a great train, and the leaders or rulers to a locomotive, which causes this human society to move towards a destination.

The laws are like the rails or tracks which provide the line to be followed by this train to a clear destination, a line which moves throughout twists and turns. It is clear that a good train must have the following conditions:

• The land which the train moves through must have sufficient strength for the greatest extent of pressure.

• The distance between the two tracks or rails must be carefully coordinated with the wheels of the locomotive as well as the walls of tunnels and the heights of the tunnels must suit the highest level of the trains.

• The ups and downs must not be so sharp that they are beyond the power of the brakes of the train.

• The possibility of landslides or floods along the way which the train moves must be carefully studied so that the train can pass through that area under all conditions.

Noting these examples, we return to human society.

A lawgiver who wants to give the best laws for human beings must have the following qualities:

1. Know the human species in a perfect and total way and be aware of all of their instincts, feelings, needs and difficulties.

2. All of the praiseworthy qualities and talents which exist in a human being should be taken into

consideration and laws should be made use of for their blossoming.

3. The events and accidents which are possible to occur should be foreseen, as well as the necessary precaution taken.

4. Such a lawgiver should have no particular interests in society so that in providing the laws, his thoughts turn upon his own interests or his family or his social group.

5. This lawgiver must allow human beings the possibility to benefit from all of the advances made as well as to learn from the deviations.

6. This lawgiver must, at the maximum, be free from error, mistakes and forgetfulness.

7. Finally, this lawgiver must have such power that no position or power in society may intimidate him and he not fears anyone. At the same time, he must be very kind and merciful.

In what person have these conditions been gathered?

Can a human being be the best lawgiver?

Has anyone understood the human being in a complete way to date? A famous scholar in our age has written a book about the human being calling it, Man: The Unknown Creature.

Have the human spirit, instincts and feelings been completely known?

Are the physical, spiritual and emotional needs of the human being clear for a person?

Can someone be found in the midst of average people who have no special benefits or interests in society?

Do you know of any human being among ordinary people who is free from error and sin and who has the awareness of all of the issues of life and individual human beings and society?

Thus, other than God and those who received the Divine revelation, there can never be a good and perfect lawgiver.

In this way, we must conclude that God Who created the human being to reach perfection must send someone as a guide to place the laws of heaven at the disposal of the human being.

It is clear that at the time when people know that laws are the laws of God, they will put them into practice with more credibility and certainty. In other words, this awareness is a valuable guarantee of those laws.

The Relationship between Monotheism and Prophethood

It is important to note the following that the system of creation is itself a living witness for the existence of the Divine prophets and their mission.

The reason is this: a short glance at this wondrous system of existence shows us that nothing of the needs of creatures is hidden from His Mercy.

For instance, if He gives us eyes with which to see, He has also given these eyes, lids and lashes so that they are protected and so that the light which enters is regulated and the eye is not harmed.

The eye has a radius which can see in several directions without the turning of the head.

Is it possible that God Who so met the needs of the human being not provide a leader and a guide who is pure and trustworthy to bring His revelation?

A famous philosopher, Abu 'Ali Sina (Avicenna) in his famous book Shifa' says:

"The needs of the human being for the sending of the prophets for the survival of the human species and their moving towards perfection is greater than their need for lashes, eyebrows and the arch of the foot; thus, is it possible for Him to provide those and not these?"

Think and Answer

1. What are the greatest needs of life of humanity?

2. Why is it that a human being cannot live without laws?

3. Give a living example to clarify the role of law in human life.

4. What qualities should the best lawgiver have?

5. Why should the prophets be of the human species?

Lesson 23: Why are the Prophets Free of Sin and Error?

Without doubt, more important than anything else, a prophet must attract the trust of the general public in such a way that his words contain no possibility of being lies or erroneous, otherwise, his position of leadership will be a shaky one.

If they are not immaculate, using the excuse that the prophets have erred, people who seek the truth from what they say will begin to doubt their invitation. It will not be accepted, or, at least, their words will not be accepted with all of their hearts.

This reason which can be called 'trustworthiness' is one of the most important reasons for their being immaculate.

In other words, how is it possible that God give His Commands for His people to follow a person who is not truthful for if this person were to err or sin, people would not follow him. If they do, they have erred and if they do not, they have weakened his position of leadership, in particular, since the position of the leadership of the prophets completely differs with the leadership of others for people receive their entire program of life from the prophets.

Because of this, we see that the great commentators speak about the verse,

> "Obey God and obey the Prophet and those charged with authority among you." (4:59)

saying that the command for Absolute obedience is because the Prophet is immaculate as well as 'being charged with authority'. The pure leaders like the Holy Prophet are referred to as 'being charged with authority'. If not, God would never give the command to unconditional obedience to them.

Another way of proving the immaculateness of the Holy Prophet in relation to any sin is that any factor of sin is condemned to defeat within the very being of the Holy Prophet.

The explanation of this is: when we turn to ourselves, we see that we, too, are immaculate in relation to some sins or evil or unacceptable deeds.

Note the following examples:

Can you find an intelligent person who thinks about eating fire or trash or filth?

Lesson 23

Can you find an intelligent person who will walk naked through the streets and bazaars?

Clearly not! If we saw such deeds from someone, we will be assured of the fact that he is no longer normal and has become insane because an intelligent person would never do these things.

When we analyze such behavior, we see that the ugliness of such deeds is so clear that an intelligent person would never even consider them.

It is here that we can imagine what this short phrase means and say that every intelligent and healthy person is "free of' unacceptable deeds.

From this stage, we take a step further. We see some people who are free from unacceptable deeds.

For instance, an aware physician and expert who knows the various kinds of microbes well is never prepared to drink the polluted water of the dirty clothes of a person who has one of the most dangerous contagious diseases whereas an illiterate person , perhaps, would be indifferent to such a thing.

With another simple example, we reach the point that however much the level of a person rises in the area of awareness, they are less likely to do evil or ugly deeds.

Taking into consideration that if a person's faith and awareness were to rise and have so much faith in God and His court of justice, so that everything that he sees is present before his eyes, such a person will be free of all sin and every ugly deed in relation to him, like walking naked through the streets, will be in our eyes only.

For such a person, the property of something forbidden is just like the flames of fire, and just like we do not put fire in our mouths, he does not put something which is forbidden into his mouth.

We can then conclude that the prophets, because of the extraordinary knowledge, awareness and faith which they have, tame the motives of sin and the most exciting factors causing sin will not prevail upon his intellect and faith. This is why we say that the prophets are immaculate; they are insured against sin.

How can the Station of Purity be a Honor?
Some people who do not understand the meaning of purity and the factors of immaculateness and being free from sin are not aware of the fact that if God

prevents one from sin and destroys the factors which cause sin, this will not be an honor for that person!

This is coercive purity and therefore is not considered to be a virtue.

But with the discussion which he had above, this issue is very clear:

The freedom of the prophets from sin in no sense is a coercive one. Rather, it is born from their strong faith and absolute certainty, their awareness and extraordinary knowledge and this is the greatest honor for them.

If an aware physician takes care of and treats a person with the worst of diseases is this a sign of his being forced to do so?

If such a person were to follow the rules of health, would this be Considered to be a virtue?

If a person, a lawyer, were to take the disgraceful considerations into effect of a dreadful crime and try to prevent it, is this a virtue?

Thus, we reach this conclusion that the fact that the prophets are free from sin is both one of their own choice and great honor for them.

Think and Answer

1. How many branches are there to being immaculate?

2. If prophets were not free from sin, what would happen?

3. What is the truth of the station of immaculateness?

4. Other than the examples given here, can you point out another example of someone who is immaculate in relation to another group?

5. Is the immaculateness of the prophets coercive or a result of free will? Why?

Lesson 24: The Best Way to come to Know the Prophets

Without doubt, accepting the claims of every pretender to prophethood is unintelligent and illogical.

It was possible that the claims to prophethood and the mission on behalf of God were true but the possibility also existed that an opportunist and a cheat was introducing himself as a prophet. Because of this, it is necessary that certain criteria be established for evaluating the claims of the prophets and their relationship with God.

In order to reach such a determination, various ways exist, the most important of which are two:

1. To study the content of the invitation of the prophets and to collect the laws and signs.

2. Miracles and deeds which exceed normal human ones.

Let us be allowed to first speak about miracles.

There are some people who are surprised by the word 'miracle' or consider miracles to be equivalent to fairy tales and myths whereas if we look carefully at the meaning of the word 'miracle', we would not get such an incorrect picture of it.

A miracle is not an act which is not possible and without reason or cause. Rather a miracle is something as simple as an interpretation of an extraordinary deed, the performance of which is beyond the means of normal people and can only be undertaken with the help from something beyond nature.

Thus, a miracle has the following conditions:

1. Something which is possible and accepted.

2. Normal people and even geniuses, by relying on the strong power of humanity cannot do the deed.

3. The miracle-maker must be so certain of what he is doing that he can challenge others to try.

4. No one else was able to offer these miracles and everyone was impotent before them.

Miracles must be connected with the claims of prophethood or imamate (thus any work which is extraordinary and comes from someone other than a prophet or pure Imam is not called a miracle, but a blessing).

Lesson 24

Several Clear Examples

Many people are familiar with the miracles of the Prophet Jesus, peace be upon him, who was able to raise the dead to life and heal the incurably sick.

Is there any clear and intelligent reason why a human being, after death, is not able to return to life?

Is there any scientific or intelligent reason why a person with an incurable disease cannot be cured?

Doubtlessly, however, the power which a human being has, under the present conditions, is not sufficient to be able to raise the dead and give them life or to treat some diseases, even if all the doctors of the world were to Work together and give each other of their experience and knowledge.

But what is to prevent a person with a divine power and with particular awareness which has come from God's endless ocean of knowledge, to be able to give life to the body of a dead person or to cure one who has an incurable disease?

Science says, "I do not know and I do not have the ability," but it would never say that it is impossible or unintelligent.

And other examples: It is not possible for any human being to journey to the moon without making use of a space ship but at the same time that there is nothing to prevent a superior force and a horse which is stronger than horses which we know to be placed at the disposal of a person and without using a space ship, that person go to the moon or planets above it.

If a person can do such an extraordinary feat, and along with that, claim prophet hood, and ask others to try and challenge everyone and everyone prove to be impotent in relation to him, we will find certainty that it is from God because it is not possible that God give such a strength to a human being who lies and would cause His creatures to be misled. (Note this with care).

Miracles Should Not be Confused with Superstitions

Extremism, of the right or the left, has always been the source of corruption and darkening of the truth.

As to miracles, this very statement is true. Whereas some pseudo intellectuals speedily and directly deny miracles, another group tries to extend miracles and take the weak traditions and fairy-tale superstitions which were most often done with the help of the enemies and mix them with miracles and the scientific visage of miracles of the prophets and cover them with fairy tale like stories and unclarities so that the real miracles of these kinds of stories not be known.

It is because of this that our great scholars were always very careful to avoid such mistakes in Islamic Traditions relating to miracles.

Also, it is because of this that the 'Science of Biography' came into being so that the methods of Traditions be known and that the correct and the weak traditions be separated from one another, and that the useless not mixed with the truth.

The policies of the colonialists and the extremists today have been busy trying to mix the pure with the impure and in this way give an unscientific image to all of them. We must be very aware of these conspiracies of the enemies.

What is the Difference Between Miracles and Extraordinary Deeds?

We have often heard that a group of ascetics have undertaken extraordinary feats. People who have seen these deeds are not few. This is a reality, not a fairy tale.

It is here that this question arises as to what difference is there between this extraordinary work and the miracles of the prophets? And what criteria should we use to separate them?

Here the question arises as to what the difference is between these extraordinary feats and the miracle of the prophets and what criteria we use to distinguish them.

This question has several responses, the two clearest of which are:

1. An ascetic always does work which is limited In other words, no ascetic is ready to do what you ask him to do. He undertakes an extraordinary feat which he himself wants to do, that is, something which he has practiced a great deal, learned how to do well and at which is an expert.

The reason for this is clear because the power or force of every human being is limited and in one or several things only can he attain skill.

But the extraordinary deeds of the prophets had no limits, no conditions to be able to perform them. They can, whenever they want, perform a miracle which is suggested to them because they receive help from the endless power of the Creator and we know that God's power is not limited, whereas the power of the human being is very limited.

2. The work done by an ascetic, another ascetic does the same thing in the same way, that is, it is not beyond the power of the human being. Because of this, an ascetic who does extraordinary feats never invites others to try and to do what he has done and he does not challenge him because he knows that in his town or in the surrounding areas, there are other individuals such as himself who can do the same thing.

But the prophets, with complete assurance and certainty, challenge others and they say, "Even if you were to bring together all of humanity, they could not do what we are doing or can do."

This difference is also true in relation to magic. These refer to the two differences which we have mentioned and they divide a miracle from magic. (Note this with care).

Think and Answer

1. Why do we call a miracle, a miracle?

2. Is a miracle an exception to the law of causes?

3. How many differences can you name between the work of the prophets and that of the ascetic and magician?

4. What is the main condition for a miracle?

5. Have you ever seen something which is similar to a miracle?

Lesson 25: The Greatest Miracle of the Prophef of Islam

All scholars of Islam believe that the Qur'an is the greatest miracle of the Prophet of Islam (S).

When we say the most superior, it is because, in the first place, the Qur'an is not an intellectual miracle but rather has to do with the spirit and intellect of the people and secondly, it is eternal and everlasting and third, it is a miracle which has cried out for 14 centuries.

It says: "If you do not believe that this is a Book of God, bring one like it" This invitation to an equivalent or something like it or challenge has appeared several times in the Holy Qur'an. In one place it says:

"Say: If the whole of humanity and jinn were to gather together to produce the life of this Qur'an, they could not produce the like thereof, even if they backed up each other with help and support." (17:88)

In another place, it has made the condition for the bringing of something like it even easier. It says:

"Bring ten suras forged like unto it and call to your aid whomever you can other than God if you speak the truth." (11: 13)

"If they (your false gods) answer not your (call), know that this Revelation is sent down (replete) with the knowledge of God..." (11:14)

"And if you are in doubt about that which We have revealed to Our Servant, then bring a surah like it and call your witnesses, other than God, if you are truthful." (2:23)

In the next verse, it directly states:

"But if you do not and you shall never do — guard yourselves against the fire." (2:24)

These continuous and successive invitations to challenge the Qur'an show that the Holy Prophet placed the greatest of emphasis and importance upon the miracle of the Qur'an even though many other miracles have been recorded about the Prophet and have appeared in books on Islamic history.

As the Holy Qur'an is a living miracle, we will, in this discussion, give greater emphasis to it.

How they have remained impotent in face of this challenge It is interesting that the Holy Qur'an places the greatest emphasis upon inviting the opponents to the arena and with stimulating comparisons, it challenges them to enter the arena so that no excuse remain for anyone.

Words like, "If you speak the truth...", "You can never do so...", "Even if you seek help from all of humanity...", "Bring at least one verse like it...", "If you become a kafir, a flaming fire is awaiting you..." speak of this truth.

These are all on one side. On the other side, the struggle of the Holy Prophet with the opponents was not a simple struggle, because Islam not only endangered their religion which they firmly supported, but also endangered their economic, political interests and even their very existence.

In other words, the progress and influence of Islam caused all of the lives to be turned upside down. Thus, they were obliged to come to the arena with all of their power and force.

No matter what the cost, in order to disarm the Holy Prophet, they would have to bring a verse like a verse of the Holy Qur'an so that they could no longer rely on the Qur'an as a miracle, and everyone who believed in it would become defective and it would become a document for proving their truth.

They invited all of the Arabs who were learned scholars to help them but every time that they tried to challenge the Holy Qur'an, they were defeated and they very readily retreated. The story of these events have been recorded in the history books.

The Story of Walid ibn Mughayrah

Among the people invited to this challenge was Walid ibn Mughayrah from the Bani Makhzum who was famous at that time among the Arabs for his literary abilities.

They asked him to think about this challenge and to give his opinion about the miraculous verses of the Qur'an and its extraordinary influence.

Walid asked the Holy Prophet to recite a verse of the Holy Qur'an for him. The Holy Prophet recited a verse from Surah Ha Mim (as-Sajdah, n.32).

This verse caused such excitement in Walid that he, without thinking, arose from his place and left the group of the Bani Makhzum which had been formed, saying, "I swear by God that I have heard words from Muhammad which neither resembled the words of human beings nor the fairies."

"His words have a special tone and a particular beauty. They are like a branch of a tree which bears a great deal of fruit; they are words which are victorious over all things and nothing will be victorious over them." These words caused the Quraysh to whisper among themselves, "Walid has lost his heart to Muhammad."

Abu Jahl, in a state of anxiety, went to his home and told him what the Quraysh were saying. He invited him to a meeting of theirs.

Walid went to their group and said, "Do you think Muhammad is crazy? Have you seen the effects of insanity in him?"

Those who were present said, "No."

"Do you think that he is a liar? Was he not famous to date among you for his truthfulness and his trustworthiness? Did you not call him a truthful and trustworthy person?"

Some of the leaders of the Quraysh said, "Then what should we call him, what should we relate him to?"

Walid thought a bit and then said, "He is a magician."

Even though they tried to turn the common people away from the Qur'an, which they were attracted to, this commentary of 'magic' was itself living proof of the extraordinary attraction of the Holy Qur'an and they called this attraction, bewitchment while it had nothing to do with magic.

It was because of this that the Quraysh spread this opinion everywhere that Muhammad is a magician and these verses are his magic, keep away from him and try not to listen to what he is saying. But in spite of all of their efforts and endeavors, their plan had no effect. The thirsty were everywhere and plentiful. They had pure hearts and group by group, they joined the Qur'an. They drank of the pure water of the heavenly message and the enemy, defeated, retreated.

The Holy Qur'an, today, challenges all of the people of the world and invites them to struggle against it. It cries out, "If you doubt the truth of these verses and you think that it is born of human thought, bring its like. O scholars, philosophers and literary persons, writers from whatever nation or people!"

We also know that the enemies of Islam, in particular, Christian priests, who know Islam to be a revolutionary school, full of meaning, a strong competitor and a danger to it, every year spend millions of dollars to spread anti-Islamic propaganda.

They are active in Islamic countries under the cover of culture, science and health. What would happen if they made the way closer, if they were to invite Arab-Christian scholars, poets, writers and philosophers to write verses like the verses of the Holy Qur'an to silence the Muslims?

It is clear that if such a thing were possible, at whatever the cost, they would do so.

The very fact that they are unable to do so is a proof before the opponents and proof of the miracle of the Qur'an.

Think and Answer

1. Why is the Holy Qur'an the highest and most superior of the miracles of the Holy Prophet?

2. How does the Qur'an challenge people?

3. Why have the enemies of the Qur'an referred to it as magic?

4. Why is Islam a strong opponent for present clay?

5. What was the story of Walid ibn Mughayrah?

Lesson 26: A Glance at the Miracle of the Qur'an

What do the letters stand for at the beginning of some of the Surahs?

We see that the beginning verse of many of the surahs of the Holy Qur'an are letters, like alif lam mim, alif lam mim rah and ya sin.

One of the secrets and the philosophy behind these letters, according to some of the Islamic traditions, is that God is showing the great miraculous and eternal quality of the Holy Qur'an.

That is, how can the Qur'an make use of these simple letters and create such words which are greater than the letters while every child can repeat them and in truth the appearance of this important fact is one of the most important miraculous issues.

Now this question arises. From what point of view is the Qur'an a miracle? It is only because of its simplicity and tone, or, in other words, the sweetness and clarity of its expression and the extraordinary influence of it or is it because of something else?

The truth is that whenever we look at the Holy Qur'an from different points of view, each one presents another image of its miracle. For instance:

1. Eloquence: The sweetness and extraordinary attraction of the miraculous words and concepts.

2. The expression of the highest content from every point of view, especially beliefs which lack any sort of superstition.

3. Scientific miracle: That is, the uncovering of issues which human beings during that age had not come to know.

4. To foresee and speak directly and accurately about some future events (the hidden news of the Qur'an).

5. The lack of contradiction, disputes, disorderliness and others.

A discussion about each of these five areas is very extensive but we will discuss some of them here.

Eloquence

We know that every discussion has to aspects: letter and content.

Whatever letters and words of beauty contain the necessary unity and are free of complicated and complex expression and also the sentence structure is such that they are exactly what one desires to hear and they attract the heart, that expression is called eloquence.

The Qur'an has both of these two qualities to the highest extent possible so that to date no one has been able to bring verses and surahs with such attraction, sweetness and tone.

In the previous lessons, we saw that Walid ibn Mugharayah, a skilled Arab linguist, was enraptured by hearing a verse of the Holy Qur'an and was made to think about how to express something to the Quraysh which would lessen the Holy Prophet in the eyes of the people, finally thought of the word 'bewitchment' and called Muhammad a be This is what they called the Prophet of Islam, even though they wanted, in this way, to condemn him, but, in truth, they were unable to do so.

At the same time, this calling the Prophet a magician is to admit to the extraordinary effects of the Qur'an in the sense that it cannot be explained and justified in simple terms and it must be recognized as being something miraculous.

But instead of them accepting the truth, and considering it to be a miracle, and gaining faith, they took the way of myth and legend. They were led astray and said that it was magic.

In the history of Islam, it can very often be seen that whenever harsh individuals went to see the Prophet, or hear verses of the Holy Qur'an, they changed their direction in life and allowed the light of the Holy Qur'an to guide them. This well shows that the attractions and eloquence of the Qur'an are miraculous.

We do not need to go far to see that whenever those people who are familiar with the Arabic language read the Qur'an, and they repeat it, they receive pleasure; they do not tire or become satiated.

The words of the Holy Qur'an are very accurate, are mixed with the purity of expression, and, at the same time, are clear and enlightening as well as, when necessary, they are firm.

It is necessary to point out that the Arabic language at that time had progressed a great deal as a language and examples of poetry during the Age of Ignorance, before the appearance of Islam, are among the best poems from the point of view of language.

It was famous that every year, the greatest literary men of the Hijaz would gather together and would offer the best examples of their poems in a commercial-literary center in the ukaz bazaar. One poem would be chosen as the best of the year. They would write it down and recite it in the Ka'bah. At the time of the Prophet, seven of these still existed and were called mu'alaqat sab'.

But after the descent of the Holy Qur'an, they paled in comparison to the eloquence of the Holy Qur'an, so that one after another, they were removed from there and were forgotten in history.

The commentators upon the various verses of the Qur'an express all of the wondrous qualities of the verses so that reference can be made to them to gain a familiarity with it.

A familiarity with the Holy Qur'an shows that this saying of the Prophet of Islam, is not an exaggeration, "The Holy Qur'an has a beautiful exterior and a deep and subtle interior. The wonders of the Qur'an can never be counted and the miraculous qualities of the Qur'an will never age."

The Commander of the Faithful, 'Ali, peace be upon him, a great student of the Holy Qur'an, also says in the Nahj al-Balaghah, "The spring of hearts is in the

Qur'an and it is the source of the springs of knowledge. There is no better way to remove the rust of the hearts and souls of people than through the Holy Qur'an."

Think and Answer

1. What is the philosophy behind the beginning letters of some of the verses of the Holy Qur'an?

2. Is the Holy Qur'an a miracle from only one point of view? Or from several points of view?

3. Why did the opponents of the Holy Qur'an refer to the Prophet of Islam as a 'bewitcher'?

4. What is the difference between eloquence and bewitching?

5. What age did the mu'alaqat sab' refer to and what does it mean?

Lesson 27: The World View of the Holy Qur'an

Before anything else, we should study the intellectual and cultural environment from which the Holy Qur'an arose.

From the point of view of all historians, the Hijaz was among the most underdeveloped and backward areas of the world at that time. During the Age of Ignorance, the people of this area are referred to as savage or half-savage.

From the point of view of ideology, they were very firm worshippers of idols and stone and wood statues had cast their disgraceful shadows upon all of their culture.

They even say that they made statues and idols out of dates and they would kneel before them but at times of famine, they would eat them.

They held great hatred for female children so that they buried them alive and they called the angels, the daughters of God! They thought that God was just like a human being.

They were very surprised by the idea that a person should only worship One God. When the Holy

Prophet invited them to worship the One God, with great surprise, they said,

"Has he made the gods (all) into one God? Truly this is a wondrous thing." (38:5)

Whoever spoke against their superstitions and their myths were called liars and insane.

They were ruled by a very firm tribal system and the differences and disputes among the tribes were so extensive that the wars among them never ended and time and time again, they colored each other's environment with blood, creating blood baths. They were proud of their plunder and considered it to be part of their daily activity.

The number of people who could read and write in the area of Mecca, the center of commerce, could be counted on one hand and it was very rare to find scholars among them.

Yes, in such an environment, an individual who could not read and write and who had never had a teacher, arose and brought a book which was so full of such content and meaning that after 14 centuries, the scholars are still busy with its interpretation. Every age discovers new truths in it.

The image that the Holy Qur'an gives of the world of existence is a very accurate and exact one: monotheism is presented in the most perfect form. It expresses the secrets of the Creation of the earth, the heavens, the night and day, the sun and the moon, plants and the existence of the human being — each one as a sign of the One God in the various verses and with a varied form of expression.

Sometimes, it goes into the depths of the human being and speaks about the unity of the primordial nature:

"Now, if they embark on a boat, they call on God, making their devotion sincerely (and exclusively) to Him; but when He has delivered them safely to (dry) land, behold, they give a share (of their worship to others)!" (29:65)

Sometimes it speaks of the intellect.

Sometimes it reasons from the unity of the intellect and relies upon the journey through the horizons and souls: the secrets of the creation of the earth and the heavens, animals and mountains and seas, rain and breezes and of the body and spirit of the human being.

Lesson 27

When speaking about the Qualities of God, the most interesting and the deepest form of expression is selected.

The Holy Book says:

"There is nothing whatever like unto Him..." (42:11)

"He is God. There is no god save He; the Knower of the unseen and seen; He is the Beneficent, the Most Merciful. He is God; there is no god save He; the King, the Holy, the Peace-loving, (the bestower) of conviction, the Guardian (over all), the Ever-Prevalent, the Supreme, the Great absolute! Hallowed is God from what they associate (with Him). He is God, the Creator, the Maker, the Fashioner; His are the Excellent Names; praises Him whatsoever is in the heavens and the earth; and He is the Ever-Prevalent, the All-Wise."(59:22-24)

In expressing the Knowledge of God and explaining His Unlimitedness:

And if all the trees on earth were pens and the ocean (were ink), with seven oceans behind it to add to its (supply), yet would not the Words of God be exhausted." (31:27)

"To God belongs the Face of East and the West: whichever way you turn, there is the Face of God ..." (2:115)

When words are spoken about the resurrection and it denies the polytheists:

"He says, "Who can give life to (dry) bones and decomposed ones (at that)"? Say, "He will give them life Who created them for the first time! For He is well-versed in every kind of creation! The same who produces for you fire out of the green tree when behold! You kindle therewith (your own fires)!"

Is not He who created the heavens and earth able to create the like thereof? Yea indeed! For He is the Creator supreme of skill and knowledge! Verily when He intends a thing, His Command is, be and it is!" (36:78-82)

"On that Day will (the earth) declare her tidings." (99:4)

"That Day shall We set a seal on their mouths. But their hands will speak to us and their feet bear witness to all that they did." (36:65)

"They will say to their skins: "Why bear you witness against us?" They will say. "God has given us speech, (He) Who gives speech to everything: He created you for the first time, and unto Him were you to return." (41:21)

The value of the knowledge of the Holy Qur'an and the greatness of its content and the greatness of its content and the fact that this knowledge is free from any kind of superstition will become clear when it is compared with the altered Bible and Pentateuch.

When we compare these two with each other, for instance, we see what the Pentateuch says about the creation of the human being and then what the Holy Qur'an says.

What does the Pentateuch say about the prophets and what does the Holy Qur'an says?

How does the Bible and the Pentateuch describe God? How does the Qur'an do so?

Here the difference between these two will be made clear.

Think and Answer

1. What were the particularities of the environment from which the Qur'an arose?

2. What effect did idol worship have in their thoughts?

3. What is the difference between primordial nature and reason?

4. What is the logic used by the Qur'an in describing the Qualities of the Creator? Give examples.

5. How can one better understand the content of the Holy Qur'an?

Lesson 28: The Holy Qur'an and Modern Scientific Discoveries

There is no doubt that the Holy Qur'an is not a book about natural sciences, medicine, psychology or mathematical studies.

The Holy Qur'an is a book of guidance and one which builds a human being. It mentions whatever is necessary for one to know.

We should not expect that the Holy Qur'an be an encyclopedia about the various sciences. We should seek the light of faith and guidance, piety and purity, humanness and ethics, order and law from the Holy Qur'an and it contains all of these.

But sometimes in order to reach this goal, the Holy Qur'an indicates some of the natural sciences and the secrets of creation, in particular, in its lessons on unity; it removes the veil over the secrets of the world of creation and it discloses facts which were unknown to the scholars of that era.

This expression of the Qur'an forms a complex which we call the intellectual miracles of the Qur'an. Here we will indicate some of the intellectual miracles of the Holy Qur'an.

The Holy Qur'an and the Law of Attraction

Before Newton, no one had discovered the law of gravity in a complete way.

It is famous that while Newton was sitting under a tree, and an apple fell from the tree, he began to think about the reason and said to himself, "What energy is this which attracts the apple to itself? Why did it not go up to heaven?" After many years of study, he discovered the law of gravity.

In the discovery of this law, it was proven where the order of the stars comes from, why this earth moves around the sun and why they do not fall into each other. What power is this which keeps them in their own orbit, and they do not move this way or that.

Yes. Newton discovered that the orbiting of a body causes it to flee from the center and the law of gravity causes it to return to the center and as long as these two are in balance, that is, the distance between these two bodies brings about a gravity to create a fleeing from the center and a gravity to pull it back to the center, this attraction and repulsion permits it to remain continuously in its orbit. But the Holy Qur'an, 1000 years before this event, says:

"God is He Who raised the heaven without any pillars that you can see; is firmly established on the throne. He has subjected the sun and the moon (to His Law)! Each one runs (its course) for a term appointed. He regulates all affairs, explaining the sign in detail that you may believe with certainty in the meeting with your Lord."
(13:2)

In a Tradition from Imam 'Ali ibn Musa al-Rida about this verse, he says, "Does God not say a pillar without a pillar being seen?"

The narrator says that in response to the Imam, I said, "Yes" He said, "Thus a pillar exists but you do not see it."

Can an analogy simpler than this be found to express this to simple Arab people?

In a tradition of Hadrat 'Ali we read: "These stars which are in the heavens are cities like cities on earth and every city is connected to another city by a ray of light."

Scholars today, among the astronomers, believe that there are millions of stars which are inhabited with living creatures but the details of this are still not known.

The Discovery of the Orbit of the Earth around the Sun

It is famous that the first person who discovered that the earth moves around the sun was Galileo, who lived approximately four centuries before and before that, the Egyptian scholar, Ptolemy, had said, "The earth is the center of the universe and everything revolves around it."

Galileo was reprimanded by the Catholic Church for his discovery and his denial of this discovery saved his life but finally other scholars followed up his discovery and today it is a certain scientific fact which has been proved by space flights.

In summary, the earth being the center was negated and it became clear that this was an error of our senses because we mistake the movement of the stars and planets for the movement of the earth. We are in motion and we assume that they are!

At any rate, the opinion of Ptolemy lasted for 1500 years and it influenced the thoughts of the scholars during those years, and, at the time of the descent of the Holy Qur'an, no one had the courage to speak against this view.

Lesson 28

But when we turn to the Holy Qur'an, we see:

"You see the mountains and think them firmly fixed, but they shall pass away as the clouds pass away..." (27:88)

The Qur'an speaks very clearly about the movement of the mountains whereas we see them as immovable and the analogy of their movement with that of clouds is both an indication of calmness and quietude.

If we see that instead of the movement of the earth, the movement of the mountains is mentioned, this is so that the truth of the matter be made known because it is clear that the mountains, without the earth, have no motion and the movement of them is exactly like the movement of the earth, either around itself, or around the sun or both.

Now think that at a time when all of the scholars of the world and the masses of the people thought that the earth was motionless, and believed that all of the stars and planets moved around it, the direct confrontation of this idea and the mention of the movement of the earth is a scientific miracle!

And this from a person who had never studied and who, in general, arose from an area where there were no teachers and which was considered to be very backward from the point of view of science and culture.

Is this not a proof of the Truth of this Book?

Think and Answer

1. What is meant by 'scientific miracles' of the Qur'an?

2. Who was the first person who discovered the law of gravity and in what age did he live?

3. In what verse in the Qur'an and with what analogy does it refer to the law of gravity in general terms?

4. Who said that the earth was immobile and how long did this rule human thought?

5. In what verse and sura does the Holy Qur'an refer to the movement of the earth?

Lesson 29: Another Proof of the Rightfulness of the Prophet of Islam

In order to understand the truth of the invitation of a claimant to prophethood, and his truthfulness or falsity, we have other ways in addition to the question of his miracles and this can be another living proof of the way to reach the truth which is to study the following:

1. The moral personality and social background.

2. The conditions which ruled in the area of the invitation.

3. The conditions of the time.

4. The content of the invitation.

5. The programs and means and principles and goal.

6. An evaluation of the effects of the invitation upon the area or environment.

7. An evaluation of the faith and self-sacrifices of the invitee in relation to the goal.

8. The non-compromise with deviated suggestions.

9. The speed of the effects in public opinion.

10. A study of the faithful and understanding what group they come from.

If we, in truth, study these ten subjects in relation to every claimant and if we make a file about them, we can very easily understand the truth.

Noting that has been said above, we present a very brief study of the above issues in relation to the person of the Holy Prophet, even though each one of these items requires a separate study of its own.

That which is among the particularities of the morality of the Prophet of Islam in the midst of his social activities, according to the histories written by his friends and enemies, is clear to us that he was so pure and correct that even in the Age of Ignorance, he was given the title of 'trustworthy'. History says, "When he wanted to migrate to Medina, he assigned 'Ali, peace be upon him, the task of giving back the trusts which people had placed with him."

His courage, perseverance and good conduct, his quickness and his manliness, his forgiveness in war and peace can be seen, in particular, his command of forgiveness for the people of Mecca after the victory over this city and the surrender of the blood-thirsty enemies of Islam is clear and is clear evidence of his character.

We all know that normal, average individuals even geniuses — take on the color of their environment, whether they want to or not, of course, to a lesser or greater degree.

Now let us think that a person who lived for 40 years in the midst of ignorance, idol worship, in an environment which was formed by the weave of the culture of the people with polytheism and superstition. How is it possible that the people arise to establish pure monotheism and struggle against all forms of polytheism?

How is it possible that scientific analyses develop in an environment of ignorance?

Can one believe that without divine intervention such a wondrous phenomenon would occur?

It must be seen if the manifestation of a prophet took place in every age and era when the world was going through the Middle Ages, the age of despotism, discrimination, oppressive racial and class superiority? Perhaps we should read the words of Hadrat 'Ali, who bore witness to the age before and after the appearance of Islam.

He says, "God sent the Holy Prophet during a time when the people of the world were lost and led astray; their intellects were at the disposal of their whims and lusts; their sense of honor was destroyed; the oppression of ignorance had led them astray and in the midst of ignorance and anxiety, they were lost." (The Nahj al-Balaghah, Sermon 91).

Now think about the precepts which the slogans of equality of human beings, the elimination of racial discrimination and class distinction had in relation to the situation of that time. "Surely the believers are brothers."

The content of his invitation brought unity in all areas, the elimination of oppressive privileges, the unity of humanity, a struggle with oppression, a plan for the rule of the world, defense of the deprived and the acceptance of piety and trustworthiness as the best criteria for human values.

In the area of plans to be implemented, permission was never given to make use of the concept that the goal is a means to justify the end in order to attain the sacred goals but rather sought out sacred means. He directly would say:

Lesson 29

"And let not hatred of a people incite you not to act equitably..." (5:8)

His commands to keep to moral principles even in the midst of war, not to attack civilians, not cutting down the forests and date palms, not polluting the drinking water of the enemy, good treatment of the prisoners of war are clear signs of this truth.

The effects of his invitation upon the environment were so great that the enemies were even afraid of people going near the Prophet because they saw that his attraction and influence was extraordinary. Sometimes they raised such a commotion when he spoke that the people could not hear what he was saying, to prevent his words from entering their thirsty hearts. Because of this, and to cover over the truth of what he was saying, they called him 'bewitched' and his words, 'bewitchment'. This in itself was an admittance of the strange effects of the invitation of the Holy Prophet.

An evaluation of his self-sacrifice upon the way of his invitation shows that he, more than any other person, was a believer in and faithful to the precepts which he brought.

He stood in some of the battlefields where those who had recently accepted Islam fled. He paid no attention to the enemy who often threatened him in every way possible. He retained his beliefs and never showed weakness or doubt.

Several times they tried to kill him on the excuse that he compromised with the deviates, but he never surrendered. He would say, "If you give me the sun in one hand and the moon in another and all of the planets and stars be under my dominion, I will never give up my goal and surrender."

Not only was the effect of his invitation in public opinion wondrous, the speed by which it happened was also extraordinary. Those who have studied the books of western experts on the Middle East and on Islam, are all amazed by the speed of the spread of Islam. For example, three of the most famous ones of the West who wrote, The History of Arab Civilization and Its Basis in the East, have said that this must be admitted.

They say, "With all of the efforts for the understanding of the speedy progress of Islam in the world, the fact that in less than a century it was able to spread to most parts of the known world, is still a great puzzle."

Yes. It is a puzzle that Islam was able to penetrate into the hearts of millions of people with such speed, to absorb civilizations and bring about new civilizations.

Finally, we reach the point that the enemies were a group of unbeliever leaders, oppressors and wealthy who only sought their own self-interests whereas those who found faith were most often the pure-hearted youth, from among the large group of the abased who longed for the truth and were even slaves, individuals who other than pure hearts, had no capital and who were thirsty for the truth.

From the totality of this study, which is a very extensive one, we can well conclude that this was a divine invitation, an invitation which flowed from something beyond nature, from the great Creator for the salvation of the human being from corruption and ignorance, polytheism, oppression and injustice.

Think and Answer

1. Is there any way to come to recognize the truth of a prophet other than through his miracles? What are they?

2. What is meant by the gathering of laws and what issues must be considered?

3. Can anything be understood from a comparison of the Arabs before and after Islam?

4. Express a part of that which existed in the Age of Ignorance among the Arabs, in particular, and of the world, in general.

5. Why did the enemies of Islam condemn the Prophet by calling what he said bewitchment'.

Lesson 30: The Prophet of Islam is the "Seal of Prophecy"

A Clear Meaning of 'Seal'

The Prophet of Islam is the last Prophet of God and the hierarchy of prophethood ends with him. This is one of the necessary precepts of Islam.

What is meant by necessary is that whoever joins the ranks of the Muslims must understand that all Muslims believe this and that this is among their decisive beliefs. That is, just as those who have dealings with Muslims know that they emphasize the principle of unity, they must also know that the seal of the prophethood by the Prophet of Islam is also agreed to by all and there is no group of Muslims who are in anticipation of the coming of another prophet.

In truth, the movement of humanity upon its way towards perfection has passed through various states with sending of the prophets and they have attained a level upon this way so that they can stand on their own two feet. That is, by relying upon the universal teachings of Islam, they can solve their problems.

In other words, Islam is the final law and it is the age of maturity of humanity. From the point of view of belief, it is the most perfect of contents of religious thought and from the point of view of practice, it has so been formulated that it is coordinated with every age and every generation.

The Reason for the 'Seal of the Prophecy'

In order to prove this, we have many reasons, the most clear of which are three:

1. The necessity of this issue — we have pointed out that whoever deals with Muslims, wherever in the world they may be, may come to know that they believe in the seal of prophethood with the Prophet of Islam and that if a person accepts Islam with sufficient reasons, they have no choice but to accept the ending of prophethood with him. And as in the previous lessons we have given sufficient proofs of this, we must also accept this idea, which is one of the necessities of this religion.

2. Verses of the Holy Qur'an are also clear proof of the end of prophethood with the Prophet of Islam.

"Muhammad is not the father of any of your men, but (he is) the Apostle of God and the Seal of the Prophets: and God has full knowledge of all things." (33:40)

Lesson 30

This verse was revealed when the idea of foster children was prevalent among the Arabs. They would accept a child who had a different mother and father as their adopted child and they accepted the child into their home as if it was their own child. The child was Mahram and would inherit, etc.

But Islam came and did away with this ignorant custom saying foster children are not covered by the Divine Law like real children. Among them was Zayd, the foster child of the Prophet of Islam who was considered to be a child of the Prophet.

Thus the Holy Qur'an says that you should only describe the real qualities of the Prophet which are two: Divine mission and Seal of Prophethood instead of introducing him as the father of one of these individuals.

This shows that the seal of prophethood by the Prophet of Islam was clear for all, permanent and decisive as was his mission.

The only question which remains here is, "What exactly is meant by 'seal'?"

Seal means to end something. For instance, a seal is placed at the end of a letter and if we see that sometimes a ring is called a 'seal', it is because in that age, it was used in place of the signature of a name. Whoever at the end of his letter sealed it with the ring in which his name was carved, used it as a seal and every image on the ring was particular to that person.

In the Islamic Traditions, we read, "When the Holy Prophet wanted to write a letter for the kings and leaders of these times, and invited them to Islam, his servant told him that the kings would not accept a letter unless it had a seal. The letters of the Holy Prophet to that time did not have a seal. He ordered that a ring be made for him in which was imprinted, "There is no god but God and Muhammad is the Prophet of God." The Prophet, after this, ordered that his letters be sealed with that from then on."

Thus, the meaning of seal is clear.

3. We have many traditions which prove the seal of the prophethood of the Prophet of Islam, among which are:

Among the Traditions recorded by Jabir ibn Abdullah Ansari, he records the Prophet as saying,

"Among the religions, Islam is like a house which has been built and completed and made beautiful and only one mud brick remains; whoever enters through there or looks through that, says, "How beautiful,' but this has an empty place. I am that last mud brick and all prophets end with me." *(Tafsir Majma' al-Bayan).*

Imam Sadiq says, "The permissible of Muhammad is permissible until the Day of Resurrection and the forbidden is forbidden until the Day of Resurrection." (Usul al-Kafi, volume 1, p.58).

In the famous Traditions of the Shiites and Sunnite from the Prophet, we read that he said to 'Ali,

"You are like Aaron in relation to Moses in relation to me, other than the fact that after me there will be no prophet," and tens of other Traditions.

As to the seal of the prophethood of the Prophet of Islam, there are some questions which we should turn our attention towards.

Some people say that if the sending of the Prophets was through Divine Grace, why should the people of our age be deprived of this Grace? Why do you not find a new way to guide the people of our age?

But they are negligent of one point and that is that the deprivation in our age is not because they do not merit it, but because humanity's thoughts and awareness have ended and by understanding the precepts of the Holy Prophet of Islam, they can continue them.

It is perhaps a good idea to give an example here.

The prophets, who came and brought a law or a book, were five: Noah, Abraham, Moses, Jesus, peace be upon them and Muhammad, peace and the mercy of God be upon him and his descendants. They made efforts in a particular area of the history for the guidance and perfection of humanity and this passed beyond a certain stage. The second phase of the prophets was handed over and has reached a level whereby they have found their final state and the strength to continue the way.

It is just like a five stages study program which must be followed to be completed.

If a physician does not go to school and college, it does not mean that he does not have merit, it is because of this that this amount of knowledge which he gains will help him to solve the scientific difficulties he faces.

As human society is continuously changing, how can we with the permanent laws of Islam, answer the needs of that?

Lesson 30

In response, we say that Islam has two kinds of laws: one is a series of laws which resemble permanent qualities of particular human beings, like the necessity for the belief in unity, the implementation of the principles of justice, struggle against any kind of oppression.

But another part is a series of general principles which, with other changes and by the doing away of them, they take on a new form and they answer the problems of each age.

For instance, a universal principle of Islam is: respect the agreements that you make and be loyal.

It is clear that with the passing of time, new social and commercial and political ties will be made whereby a person can answer them by taking the major principle into consideration.

We have another principle, *la zarar*, which says that any law which will harm an individual or society must be limited.

You can see to what extent these universal principles of Islam are effective in solving problems and we have many such laws in Islam.

There is no doubt that leadership is a vital part of Islam with the lack of a prophet and the occultation of his successor, the issue of leadership will be terminated. Because of the principle of the seal of prophethood by the prophet of Islam, we cannot wait in anticipation for another prophet. Does this not have harmful implications for an Islamic society?

In response, we say that for this era, the necessary things have been suggested through *vilayat-i-faqih*, the leadership of religious jurisprudents who have the necessary conditions of knowledge, piety and political awareness. The means of recognizing such a leader also has been clearly expressed in Islam. There is thus no need for concern in this area.

Thus, *vilayat-i-faqih* is the end of the line of the prophets, the leadership of a religious jurisprudent who has all of the necessary conditions so that Islamic society is not left without a guardian.

Think and Answer

1. What is the exact meaning of 'seal'?

2. How can we use the Holy Qur'an to understand the meaning of 'seal'?

Lesson 30

3. Why are the people of our age deprived of the Divine prophets?

4. How many kinds of laws are there in Islam and how do they answer our needs today?

5. Can an Islamic society exist without a leader? How can you solve the issue of leadership in our times?

Lesson 31: When did Imamology Begin?

We know that after the death of the Prophet of Islam, Muslims were divided into two groups:

One group believed that the Holy Prophet did not designate a successor to himself. This group believes that he left it up to his nation to meet and decide among themselves who their leader should be. This group is called Sunnite.

The other group believes that the Holy Prophet was infallible, immaculate and free of sin and error and had knowledge so that he could spiritually and materially lead the people and preserve the essence of Islam so that it would find continuation.

They believe that selection of such a person could only come from God through the Holy Prophet of Islam and that the Holy Prophet did this and he selected Imam 'Ali as his successor. This group is called Shiites.

Our goal in these brief discussions is to follow-up these issues by using intellectual and historic reasoning verses, of the Holy Qur'an and Traditions of the Holy Prophet.

But before we begin the main discussion, several points should be mentioned.

Will this Discussion cause Differences?

The moment that the discussion centers on imamate, some people immediately say something to the effect that, "Today is not a day for such discussions!"

Today is the day to discuss Muslim unity and any discussion about the successor to the Holy Prophet only causes differences and separation!

Today we have common enemies and we have to do something about them, namely, Zionism and eastern and western colonialism. Conflicting issues must be put aside.

But this way of thinking is completely wrong.

In the first place, that which causes differences and separation is discussions and debates which are based on prejudice, illogic and hatred.

But discussions which are logical and reasonable free of discrimination and quarreling, held in a friendly environment, not only are not a cause for differences of opinion and separation, but rather they decrease the distances and common points of belief are strengthened.

In my journey to the Hijaz, with the intention of the pilgrimage to God's House, I held many discussions with the scholars and learned Sunni men. Both of us felt that these discussions not only were not ineffective, but that they caused greater unity and understanding; they decreased the distance between the two sects and everyone washed away their prejudices.

The important thing is that which will become clear in these lessons; we have many points in common with one another and we can rely upon them in face of our Common enemy.

Sunnis are divided into four sects: Hanafis, Hanbalis, Shafi's, and Malikis. Existence of these four groups have not caused separation among them and when they, at least, accept Shi'ism as a fifth school of thought, many of the differences fall away. Recently, the great Muftis and head of the al-Ahzar University (in Cairo), Shaykh Shaltut, took an effective step and formally announced the acceptance of the Shi'ite school of thought among the Sunnis.

This was a step towards the understanding of Islam and establishing friendly relations between himself and the late Burujerdi, the great leader of the Shi'ites.

Lesson 31

Secondly, we believe that Islam is crystallized in Shi'ism. While we have respect for all of the Islamic sects, we believe that Shi'ism can better introduce the real Islam in all of its dimensions and solve the problems related to the leadership of the Islamic community.

Why should we not teach our children this school with reason and logic and if we do not do this, clearly we have committed an act of treason.

We are certain that the Holy Prophet selected his successor. What is wrong with following up this belief with reason and logic?

But in these lessons, we must be careful that the religious emotions of others are not slighted.

Thirdly, in order to destroy the principles and unity of Muslims, the enemies of Islam tell such lies and so instigate Sunnis against Shi'ites, tell so many lies and so insult Shi'ites about the Sunnis so that in some countries, in general, they have grown distant from each other.

When we discuss the issue of imamate in the method described above, and mention the points which the Shi'ites emphasize, and we use proof from the books of the Sunnis, it becomes clear that the propaganda was lies and that the common enemy has tried to poison the environment.

As an example, in one of my trips to the Hijaz, I held a meeting with one of the important religious leaders of the Sunnis. He said, "I have heard that the Shi'ites have a Qur'an which is different from our Qur'an."

I was very surprised. I said: "Proving that this was not true is very simple. I invite you or your representative to come to Iran after the hajj umrah, without any previous notification. You will see that on every street, in every bazaar or mosque or home, there are Qur'ans. We will go into any mosque that you choose, and study the Qur'ans there. So that it becomes clear that our Qur'an and yours are exactly the same. Most of the Qur'ans which we use are printed in the hijaz or in Egypt and other Islamic countries."

This very friendly conversation clearly did away with the amazing misconceptions which had been planted in the mind of one of the famous religious leaders.

The point is that a discussion on imamate, in this manner, confirms the unity of Islamic society, helps in clarifying the truths and decreasing the differences of opinion.

What is Imamate?

Imam means leader, leader of the Muslims. In the principles of belief of the Shi'ites, an immaculate or pure Imam refers to a person who is the successor to the Holy Prophet in all areas, with the difference that the Holy Prophet is the founder of the school and the Imam is the guardian and preserver of it. Revelation was revealed to the Holy Prophet but not to the Imams. They learned from the Holy Prophet and they had an extraordinary knowledge.

From the point of view of Shi'ism, an immaculate Imam does not just mean leader of Islamic rule, but rather, includes spiritual and material, internal and external leadership as well. In other words, they are responsible for leadership on all levels; they are responsible for the preservation and guardianship of Islamic beliefs and ideology, without any errors or deviation and they are the selected people of God.

But the Sunnis do not see imamate in this way. They only understand imamate as leader of the rule of Islamic society. In other words, leadership in every age and time is the caliph of the Prophet and the Imam of the Muslims!

Of course, in the future lessons we will prove that in every age and era, there must be a divine representative; a prophet or a pure Imam must be upon the earth to preserve the precepts of truth and guide those who long for the truth.

If one day this person is hidden from the people, a person, as his representative, is responsible for the preservation of the precepts and the formation of a government.

Think and Answer

1. What is the reason behind people saying that to day is not a day to hold such discussions about imamate?

2. In response to this, how many answers can you give for the necessity of this discussion?

3. How does the enemy cause disputes among the Muslims and what is the way to seal these breaks?

4. Can you recall an example of a dispute which is caused by the enemy?

5. What is the meaning of imamate in Shi'ism and what is the difference with the definition given by the Sunnis?

Lesson 32: The Philosophy of the Existence of Imams (Guides)

The discussion which we had about the necessity for sending of the Holy Prophet by God, makes us familiar, to a certain extent, with the necessity for the existence of an Imam after the Prophet because in many of the important issues, they hold things in common, but here it is important to mention other reasons, as well.

Spiritual Perfection along with Divine Leadership

Before anything else, we must seek out the goal for the creation of human beings which is the highest creature of the world of Creation.

They take a way which is long and full of twists and turns towards God, towards Absolute Perfection, towards spiritual perfection in all dimensions.

Without doubt, this way cannot be taken and the goal cannot be attained without the presence of a pure leader and it is not possible to undertake this way without a leader who is a heavenly teacher because: It is a way full of darkness and the dangers of becoming lost.

It is clear that God created the human beings with their own free will and choice and gave them a conscience and a heavenly book and sent his prophets to them but it is possible that the human being, in spite of all of these facilities and possibilities, err upon the way.

Clearly, the presence of an infallible leader will help to prevent the danger of deviation and going astray to a great extent, and in this way, all existence of the Imam is necessary to complete the goal of creation of human beings.

This is that very thing which is called the 'law of kindness'. What is meant by this is that God, the Wise, has seen to all of the affairs of the human being to reach the goal of creation among which is the sending of the prophets and the selection of pure Imams, otherwise there would be an imperfection in purpose. (Note this carefully).

Guardian of the Heavenly Laws

We know that the Divine religions, at the time of their descent to the prophets, are like a drop of rain water, pure, life-giving and nurturing, but the moment one enters an environment which is polluted and brains become weak or impure, gradually they are polluted and superstitions are added to them so that the purity of the first day is lost; in this state, neither do they have attractions, nor any educational effects, nor do they quench the thirst, nor do they blossom forth in flowers of virtue.

It is here that an infallible leader must always act as a guardian of the authenticity of a school, and the being pure of the religious programs alongside it so that they guard against any deviation, extremism, alien ideas and superstitions because if religious precepts be without such a leader, in a very short period of time, they will lose their authenticity and sincerity.

For this reason, 'Ali, peace be upon him, in his Sermon 147 in the Nahj al-Balaghah says, "Yes. The earth will never be empty of a person who has arisen with the proof of God, whether through appearing of being known or being hidden, so that the Divine proof and signs not be falsified."

In truth, the heart of Imam, peace be upon him, is just like a safety deposit box in which important documents are always placed, so that they be preserved against thieves and other accidents and this is another reason for the existence of the Imam.

The Political and Social Leadership of the Ummah

Doubtlessly, no social group or gathering can continue to be alive if it is not led by a strong leader. Because of this, from the earliest times to the present, all tribes and nations have selected a leader for themselves who was, sometimes, a good person and very often, not so.

It was often the case that by making use of the needs of the ummah for a leader, a tyrant, who had coercion and who deceived the people, was imposed upon them and he took the power in hand.

On the other hand, in order for human beings to be able to reach spiritual perfection, they must take this way, not alone, but with a group or a society because the power of an individual from the intellectual, physical, material and spiritual point of view, is very limited whereas the power of a group is very strong.

But for a society, it is necessary that a correct system rule over it and human talents blossom to struggle against deviations, preserve the rights of all individuals and for reaching this great goal, programming and organization is necessary and the motives be mobilized for motion in a free environment in all of society.

It is a fact that human beings sin. Because of this, human beings have always born witness to the political deviation of the world. The necessity for a pure leader, sent on behalf of God Almighty to supervise this important issue and, also, making use of the people's power and the great thoughts of scholars, prevents any kind of deviation.

This is another of the philosophies behind the existence of the Imam and another, we repeat, is to be a guide.

Thus the duty of the people at the special times when the pure Imam is in occultation has become clear and, with the will of God, we will speak about it in later lessons.

The Necessity of the Final Proof

Not only must the heart be guided by the rays of the existence of the Imam, and follow its way towards absolute perfection, but for those who knowingly and consciously follow the wrong way and who have gone astray, there must be a final proof so that if they are promised a chastisement, it will not be without reason and no one can complain that no one had showed them the way and if they had been shown, they would not have gone astray.

In other words, it is to close the way to excuses that the proof of the truth is given to the necessary extent, and awareness is given to the unaware and to the aware, to gain strength of will power.

The Imam is a Great Intermediate for Divine Grace

Many of the scholars — following the Islamic Traditions — compare the existence of the Prophet and the Imam in human society in the total world of Creation to the existence of a heart in the body of the human being.

We know that when the heart beats, blood is sent to all the parts of the body and it nurtures all of the cells of the body.

Because the pure Imam, in the form of a perfect human being and leader of human society, is the cause for the descent of Divine Favor or Grace, and every individual, to the extent of their being in touch with the Prophet, and the Imam, can benefit from this Grace or Favor, and the Imam benefits from this very Grace, it must be said that to the same extent that the existence of the heart is necessary for a human being, the existence of this in intermediate for Divine Grace is also necessary for the activities of the world of humanity. (Note this with care).

Let it not be mistaken. The Prophets and Imams have nothing of themselves to give to others, that whatever is given is given by God, but just like the heart is an intermediate for the transmission of Divine Grace to the body. The Prophets and Imams, also, are intermediates for Divine Grace for human beings in all groups.

Think and Answer

1. What is the role of the Imam, peace be upon him, in the spiritual perfection of the human being?

2. What is the role of the Imam, peace be upon him, in the guarding of the Divine Law?

3. What is the role of the Imam, peace be upon him, in the issue of leadership of rule and the system of society?

4. What does 'final proof' mean and what role does the Imam play in this?

5. What does the intermediation of Grace mean? What is the best analogy which can be given for the role of the Prophets and Imams from this point of view?

Lesson 33: The Conditions and Special Qualities of the Imam

Before anything else, in the discussion of this issue, we must note ore necessary point and that is that:

It can clearly be seen in the Holy Qur'an that the position of leadership is the highest station that a human being can possibly attain and that it is even higher than the station of Prophethood and having a Divine mission because in the story of Abraham, the idol destroyer, peace be upon him, it says,

"And remember that Abraham was tried by his Lord with certain commands which he fulfilled: He said, "I will make thee a leader to the nations." He pleaded, "And also (Imams) from my offspring?" He answered, "But My promise is not within the reach of evil-doers." (2:124)

In this way, Abraham, after moving through the station of prophethood and his Divine mission and victory in the various Divine tests made of him, is then given the valuable position of external and internal, material and spiritual leadership of the people.

The Prophet of Islam, peace and the mercy of God be upon him and his descendants, also, in addition to the position or station of prophethood and mission,

Lesson 33

has the station of leadership and imamate as well. Others among the prophets also had this station. This is one point to note.

On the other hand, we know that the conditions and qualities necessary for the receiving of any position relate to the duties and responsibilities which a person must perform in that position or station. That is, however much the station is elevated, the responsibilities are heavier and greater, in the same proportion, the conditions and qualities necessary for the position are greater.

For instance, in Islam, a person who has the responsibility to judge and even to bear witness and becomes the congregational prayer leader must be just. When the necessity for bearing witness arises or the duty to recite the Surah Hamd and another verse in the congregational ritual prayer, justice is necessary, it is clear what conditions are honored in order to reach the position or station of imamate, with the extraordinary importance which it has.

In general, the following conditions are vital for an Imam.

An Imam, must, like a Prophet, have the station of purity, that is, be free of sin and error, otherwise he cannot lead and be a model for the people and receive the trust of society.

The Imam must consume the heart and soul of the people and his command be accepted without questioning.

A person who has sinned can never receive such trust and from all points of view, be trusted and confirmed.

How can a person who in his daily life commits errors, have his opinions be relied upon in the work of society and be followed without questioning.

Doubtlessly, a prophet must be immaculate and this quality is necessary for the Imam as well, as we pointed out above.

This can be proven in another way as well. That is 'the law of kindness' which the existence of the prophet and Imam relies upon requires the infallibility of the prophet or Imam and the mission which we pointed out in the last lesson, will be incomplete.

Lesson 33

Overflowing with Knowledge

The Imam, like a Prophet, is a place of refuge of knowledge for the people. He must know all principles and practices of the religion, the external and internal meanings of the Holy Qur'an, the Traditions of the Prophet and whatever relates to Islam, and, in a complete way, be aware because he is the preserver and guardian of the Divine Law as well as the leader and guide of the people.

A person who when a complicated issue is presented either becomes conscious or asks another person for the answer, their knowledge and information will not answer the needs of an Islamic society. They can never be given the position or station of imamate and leadership of the people.

In conclusion, the Imam must be the most aware and most knowledgeable person in relation to the religion of God after the death of the Holy Prophet who does not allow Islam to deviate.

Courage

An Imam must be the bravest individual of Islamic society because without that courage of the leader, it is not possible to accept him as leader.

He must have courage in face of the difficult events of life and sudden and unexpected happenings, courage before those who use coercion and who are oppressive and courage before external and internal enemies of Islam.

Austerity

We know that those who are captives of the gold and attractions of this world, are easily deceived and it is possible that they deviate from the way of truth and justice.

Sometimes this happens by way of greed and sometimes by way of threats, whereby the captive of this world is deviated from the straight path.

Imam must be above the possibilities of gifts of this world and not to be a captive to it.

He must be free from any chains or bonds of the material world, from all whims and lusts, from any ambition, from wealth and position so that he cannot be deceived and influenced and he then surrender and compromise because of these desires.

Ethical or Moral Attractions

The Holy Qur'an says about the Holy Prophet:

"It is part of the Mercy of God that you deal gently with them. Were you to be severe or harsh- hearted, they would have broken away from about thee." (3:159)

Not only the Holy Prophet, but the Imam and any leader of society are in need of goodness so that the people are magnetized towards him.

Without doubt, any kind of harshness and evil intentions towards the people for the Prophet and Imam is a great defect and they are free from any such defect, otherwise, many of the philosophies of existence would not be fulfilled.

These are the most important conditions which the great Ulama have mentioned for the Imam to have.

Of course, in addition to these five qualifies mentioned above, there are other qualities in the Imam, as well, but we have just mentioned the most basic ones.

Think and Answer

1. Why is the station of leadership of the highest station of a human being?

2. Why do the Prophet of Islam and other prophets who brought a divine law have the station of leadership or imamate?

3. If the Imam is not immaculate, what problem will arise?

4. What is all abundance of knowledge necessary for the Imam to have?

5. For what reason must the Imam be brave, austere and the most pure from the point of view of attracting the ethics of the people?

Lesson 34: Who has to Select the Imam?

A group of Muslims (Sunnis) believe that the Prophet of Islam (S) died not having selected his successor and they believe that this responsibility belongs to Muslims themselves to select their leader.

They undertake this act through Ijma (consensus) which is one of the reasons given in the Divine Law.

They add that this program was implemented the first time for the first caliph who was selected with the consensus of the Ummah.

And he selected the second caliph and introduced him as such.

And the second caliph selected a council of six people to select the person who should succeed him.

This Council consisted of: Imam 'Ali, peace be upon him, Uthman, Abdal Rahman ibn Awf, Talha, Zubayr and Sa'd bin Abi Waqas.

This Council, with a majority of Sa'd ibn Waqas, Abdal Rahman and Talha voted for Uthman. (The second caliph had directed that if the Council should be divided three to three, the side that Abdal Rahman ibn Awf ('Uthman's son-in-law) was on would be the person selected).

Towards the end of Uthman's reign, the people arose against him for several reasons and before he had a chance to select his successor or select a Council, he was killed.

At this time, the majority of the people turned to 'Ali, peace be upon him, and selected him as their caliph.

They pledged their allegiance to him as the successor of the Prophet, other than Mu'awiyah who was the governor of Damascus and who was certain that Imam 'Ali would not support him. He then raised the flag of opposition which was the beginning of disgraceful events in the history of Islam and caused the shedding of the blood of a great many innocent people.

Here, in order to intellectually and historically clarify what happened, several questions arise, a few of which will be mentioned here below.

Can the Ummah select the successor to the Prophet?

The answer to this question is that if we take the meaning of imamate to be external leadership of an Islamic society, the selection of a leader on behalf of society with the vote of the people is possible.

Lesson 34

But if we take imamate to mean that which we have previously mentioned and as the Holy Qur'an has described, doubtlessly, no one other than God can chose the Imam and the caliph.

The conditions for imamate, according to the commentaries on the Holy Qur'an, is knowledge of all of the principles and practices of Islam, a knowledge whose base is in heaven and relies upon the knowledge of the Prophet so that he can guard and preserve the Divine Law of Islam.

Another condition is that Imam must be immaculate and infallible, free from sin and error and is the selected of the Divine immaculateness so that the station of imamate and spiritual and material, external and internal leadership of the imamate can be assumed as well as austerity, piety, courage which is necessary to confirm this important post.

The discrimination of these conditions can clearly only be done through God and the Prophet. It is He Who knows in whose spirit immaculateness has shown its rays, and it is He Who knows who has the highest knowledge needed for leadership, the sufficient courage and spiritual strength.

Those who placed the selection of the Imam and the caliph of the Prophet in the hands of the people, in truth, changed the meaning of imamate in the Holy Qur'an and limited it to meaning only leadership and giving organization to the affairs of this world of the people. Otherwise the conditions of imamate in the general and complete sense can only be determined by the Creator and it is He Who knows who has these qualities.

The Holy Prophet, as well, could not have been selected by the vote of the people, but must rather have most definitely been selected by God Almighty, because other than God, no one can discern the necessary qualities in the Prophet.

Did the Prophet not select a Person to succeed him?

There is no doubt that the precepts of Islam were universal and eternal and according to the direct verses of the Holy Qur'an, special to no time or place.

There is, also, no doubt that at the time of the death of the Holy Prophet, the precepts of Islam had not moved beyond the Arabian peninsula.

On the other hand, 13 years of the life of the Prophet in Mecca were spent in struggle against polytheism and idol worship and 10 years of the life of the Prophet, which began from the time of the migration to Medina which was the period of the blossoming of Islam, was spent mainly in conflicts and wars imposed upon him by the enemies.

Even though the Holy Prophet spent night and day endeavoring to have Islam be better understood and to teach the precepts of Islam, but is it clear that many of the Islamic issues needed more time and a person similar to the Holy Prophet was needed to be able to do so and to accept this heavy responsibility.

Beyond this, the foreseeing of future events and providing the preliminaries for the school was among the most important tasks which was something that every leader thought about and would never allow himself to forget.

Beyond this, the Prophet of Islam had provided commands for all of the affairs of life from the most simple possible. Could it be, then, that he would not have provided for the important issue of the person who was to succeed him and not determine the imamate for the Muslims?

The totality of these three directions are clear reasons why the Prophet (S) most certainly took steps for the determination of his successor which we will mention in the later lessons so that this logical reality will become more clear, because the

Holy Prophet was never negligent in this area even though many political waves, after the Prophet, tried to fill the people's minds with the idea that he had neglected to select a successor.

Can one really believe that considering that when the Holy Prophet left the city for just a few days for a conflict (like Tabuk), he did not leave Medina empty of his successor and he took steps to assign a person to succeed him and act in his place, he not guarantee the future generations after his death by selecting his successor but rather left the Ummah in the middle of an abundant number of groups who had differences of opinion on the method of the continuity of Islam?

It is clear that the lack of assigning a successor would have been a great error for Islam which was recently formed and developing. Our intellect and logic tells us that such a situation is impossible to have come from the Prophet of Islam.

Those who say that this was the responsibility of the Ummah must at least show that the Prophet directed this issue whereas no such proof of this is offered.

Lesson 34

Consensus and Council

Let us assume that the Prophet of Islam ignored this vital issue and the Muslims themselves were duty-bound to choose his successor, but we know that consensus means the consensus of the Muslims and such a consensus did not exist in relation to the first caliph.

Only a group of the Companions who lived in Medina made the decision to do this and the rest of the cities of Islam were not in agreement and did not participate in this decision. In Medina itself, 'Ali, peace be upon him, and a large number of the Bani Hashim, did not participate in any way. Thus, such a consensus cannot be accepted as such.

And if this method be correct, why did the first caliph not use the same method in choosing the second caliph?

Why did he personally select his successor? If the determination of one person is sufficient, the Holy Prophet, who was of the highest station should have his method of selection be accepted and if the later allegiance of the people would solve this problem, in relation to the Holy Prophet, they solve it better.

Beyond this, a third difficulty arises as to the third caliph and that is why did the second caliph not use the method which was used to select the first caliph? Why did he ignore it as well as the tradition which had been used in his own case, that is, neither did he choose Consensus nor did he chose election of an individual but chose a council to do so.

If a council or the idea of consultation is correct, then why just six people? And how can the vote of three people out of six be sufficient?

These are questions which arise for every scholar of Islamic history and they have remained unanswered showing that the way to select the Imam was none of these.

Ali ibn Abu Talib was the Most Worthy of All

Let us assume that the Prophet of Islam (S) did not determine who was to succeed him. Let us also assume that it was the responsibility of the people but can it be that at the time of choosing a person, from the point of view of a person who has knowledge and piety and other qualities, and is superior to all others, be put aside and that a person who is lower on this ladder be chosen?

A large group of Islamic scholars, even those who are among the Sunnis, have directly stated that 'Ali, peace be upon him, was the most aware person of

Lesson 34

Islamic affairs and the Traditions and traces which have remained from him, bear witness to this truth.

The history of Islam says that he was a place of refuge for the Ummah in all intellectual knowledge and difficulties and even if the other caliphs were asked difficult and complicated questions, they asked 'Ali to answer them.

His courage, piety and austerity and other outstanding qualities which he possessed were superior to those of any other. Thus, if we assume that the people should select the most superior person, 'Ali, peace be upon him, was the most deserving.

(Of course, this discussion has many, many documents which are beyond the range of this brief study to be presented here. Students who are interested may study further in this area).

Think and Answer

1. Why can the people not select and choose the successor to the Prophet?

2. Does our intelligence and logic tell us that the Prophet did not select any one to succeed him or not?

3. What method was used to choose the first three caliphs?

4. Was their method of selection based on Islamic precepts and logic?

5. Why was 'Ali the most deserving of all?

Lesson 35: The Qur'an and Imamate

The Qur'an, this great heavenly book of ours is the best guide in all areas and in the area of imamate, also, it presents the issue from its various dimensions.

The Qur'an says that Imamate comes from God

Just as we previously showed in the story of Abraham, peace be upon him, the Qur'an refers to the state of imamate and leadership of Abraham, peace be upon him, to follow the stage of prophethood, Divine mission and passing the difficult tests presented to him. It says:

"And remember that Abraham was tried by his Lord with certain commands which he filled. He said, "I will make you an Imam to the nations." (2:124)

The Holy Qur'an and various histories show that he attained this stage after struggling with the idol worshippers of Babel, his migration to Damascus, his building of the Ka'bah and taking his child, Isma'yl, to the place of sacrifice.

If prophethood and the Divine mission must be determined by God, imamate and leadership must also be determined by God for it relates to all aspects of the human being and it is to help direct them towards perfection. This is not something that the people may do. The Holy Qur'an says:

> "I will make You an Imam to the nations." (2:124)

In another verse it says,

> "And We made them leaders guiding (men) by Our Command and We send them Inspiration."(21:73)

Similar, to this, it can be shown in other verses of the Qur'an that God must select Imam and beyond this, at the time when we read that Abraham asked that his offspring be included, he was told:

> "But My promise is not Within the reach of wrong doers." (2:124)

It says that his prayer will be answered but those who had committed oppression would never reach this high station.

Noting the fact that an oppressor, both in the meaning of the word as well as the logic of Qur'an, has an extensive meaning, including the clear and hidden sins of polytheism and any kind of oppression against other people and noting that only God can know this in a complete and perfect way, because only God is aware of what goes on inside people, it is clear that only God can select the person for this stage.

The verse on Preaching the Mission

"O, Prophet, Proclaim the (Message) which has been sent to thee from your Lord. If you do not, you would not have fulfilled and proclaimed His Mission. And God will defend you from men (who corrupt) for God guides not those who reject Faith." (5:67)

The tone of this verse shows that the assignment is a heavy one which has been placed upon the Prophet's shoulders. He was anxious about the mission which might possibly meet up with opposition from the people.

Thus the verse tells the Prophet that God commands the endeavors to have Islam be better understood and give him security and that he will be protected.

This important issue clearly does not relate to monotheism and polytheism in the struggle with the enemies from among the Jews and hypocrites, etc. because at the time of the revealing of this verse, this issue had been completely solved.

And, also, the announcing of the normal precepts of Islam did not have these dangers. From the external interpretation of the verse, it can be seen that it was a command which was of the same weight as the Divine mission. That is, if endeavors were not made, the truth of the Divine mission would not have been expressed.

Can this command, then, be anything other than the selection of the successor to the Prophet? In particular, since the verse was revealed at the end of life of the Holy Prophet and it relates to the issue of the caliphate, which is the continuation of the issue of prophethood and the Divine mission of the Holy Prophet.

In addition, there are many Traditions recorded from a large group of the Companions of the holy Prophet including Zayd ibn Arqam, Abu Sa'id Khudri, ibn 'Abbas, Jabir Abdallah Ansari, Abu Hurayrah, Hudaifah and ibn Ma'sud.

Some of these Traditions have come to us through eleven ways and a large number of them are from the Sunni scholars, both - these who transmit the Traditions, historians as well as recorders which say that the above verse was about 'Ali, peace be upon him, and that it was revealed on the day of Ghadir. (For further information, see the books Ahqaq al-Haqq, al-Qadir, al-Marja'at and Dalail al-Sadaq).

We will discuss the events of Ghadir, with the Will of God, in the section on Traditions but here we will simply remind ourselves that this is a clear sign because the Prophet of Islam was duty- bound to announce on the return from his last hajj and at the end of his life that he had officially selected 'Ali, peace be upon him, as his successor and introduce him to the people.

The Verse on Obedience to the Commanders

"O you who believe! Obey God and obey the Prophet and those charged with authority among you..." (4:59)

Here, the command to obey 'those charged with authority' directly follows the obedience to God and the Holy Prophet.

Does it mean 'those charged with authority' as leaders and rulers in every age and in every environment? But are Muslims of each age and in each country obliged to follow the commands of the leaders without question (as some of the Sunnis say)?

This does not agree with any kind of logic because most of the leaders, in the various ages, were deviated, polluted, affiliated and oppressive.

Does this verse say to obey the rulers upon the condition that they are not rulers against the precepts of Islam?

This also does not fit with the generalization of the verse.

Does it mean that they are only to obey the Companions of the Prophet? This also does not agree with the extensiveness mentioned in the Holy Qur'an to include all ages and times.

Thus we can conclude that which is meant by the infallible leaders who exist in every age and in every era, obedience of whom is unconditional and obligatory and his commands, like the commands of God and the Prophet, must be carried out.

There are many Traditions in Islam in this area and the fact that those charged with authority has been related to 'Ali or the infallible Imams is further proof of this. (For further information see the Tafsir Nemunah, vol. 3, p.435).

The Verse of Leadership (Wilayat)
"Your (real) leaders are (no less than) God, His Apostle and the (fellowship of) believers those who establish regular prayers and regular charity when they bow down humbly (in worship)." (5:55)

The Qur'an relies upon the word innamah which in Arabic refers to exclusiveness: the Wali and leader of the Muslims is exclusive to three people: God, the Holy Prophet and those who have found faith and who pay the zakat at the time of the ruku'.

There is no doubt that what is meant by leadership is not the friendship of Muslims with one another because friendship with one another does not need to have the word unconditional added to it.

All Muslims are friends with each other even though, at the time of the ruku', zakat is not paid. Thus wilayat' here means the spiritual and material leadership, in particular, since it is placed along side the wilayat of God and the wilayat of the Prophet.

This point is also clear that the above verse, with the situation in which it appears, refers to a particular person who has paid the zakat while in the state of ruku' because otherwise it is not necessary that one pay the zakat while in that state; this is a sign, not a description.

The totality of this, then, shows that the above verse refers to the meaningful story of 'Ali, peace be upon him, in particular, since he was in the midst of the ruku' when a needy person came to the mosque of the Prophet to seek help.

No one answered the needy person but in that state, 'Ali, peace be upon him, with his right hand, indicated his finger with a ring on it. The needy person took the valuable ring. The Prophet saw what was going on with the corner of his eye.

After his ritual prayer ended, he raised his head and said, "God! The brother of Moses has asked that you extend his spirit and make things easy for him and cut the difficulty of his tongue, and have Aaron be his helper and assistant... O God! I am Muhammad, the Prophet, and the person you selected, opened my chest and made my work easy and from among my family, have 'Ali be my helper so that through him, my back will be strong and firm..."

The Prayer of the Holy Prophet had not as yet ended when Gabriel appeared and revealed the verse above.

It is interesting to note that many of the recorders of the Traditions who are famous Sunnis, and their historians and commentators, say that this verse refers to Hazrat 'Ali and more than 10 of the Companions of the Holy Prophet.

There are many verses about wilayat but we have only mentioned four verses in relation to this issue.

Think and Answer

1. According to the Holy Qur'an, who is to select the Imam?

2. When was the command to endeavor to have Islam be better understood revealed and what is the content of it?

3. In relation to what person is it reasonable to have unconditional obedience?

4. For what reason does the verse, "*Your (real) friends are (no less than) God,*" (5:58) refer to the leader ship and imamate?

5. In all of the verses of the Qur'an about the issue of wilayat', what point can be made?

Lesson 36: Imamate in the Traditions of the Holy Prophet

When we study the Traditions of Islam written in books, in particular the books of the Sunnis, a researcher encounters an abundance of Traditions of the Holy Prophet which prove the station of the imamate and vicegerency of 'Ali, peace be upon him.

Researchers are surprised that with ail of these Traditions, any doubt should remain on the issue, much less that a person would want to chose a way that is different from the way of the Ahlul Bayt.

These Traditions, which reach into the hundreds (like the Tradition of Ghadir), and tens of other Traditions recorded in tens of famous books are so clear that if one were to follow them, even if one were to put aside following the dictates of a religious authority, the issue would still be so clear that no further proof would be necessary.

As an example, several famous Traditions in this area will be presented and or those who wish to study further in this area, we will mention the sources in which they may do so. (See al-Maraj'at and al-Ghadir).

Lesson 36

The Tradition of Ghadir

Many of the historians of Islam have written that the Holy Prophet of Islam, towards the end of his life, after the ritual pilgrimage (hajj), spoke to many of the old and new Muslims who, in faith, had come from all over the Hijaz region to perform this ritual, at the time of the return from Mecca, in the area of Jufah, between Mecca and Medina, when they reached a wilderness known as Ghadir Khum, which was a crossroads which separated the people of the Hijaz.

Before the Muslims separated from each other to each go to their particular area of the Hijaz, the Prophet ordered his followers to stop. Those who were ahead were invited to return and those who had remained behind, caught up with them.

The weather was very hot and burning. There was no roof to shelter them. The Prophet informed them that they should all gather to listen to a new command from God which would be expressed during a sermon.

A pulpit was prepared by saddles placed upon a camel and the Holy Prophet mounted the pulpit and addressed the gathering.

"I will soon accept God's invitation (to death) and I will leave you. I am responsible and you are responsible. How will you bear witness to me?"

The people said, "We swear that you have carried out your mission and that you have done your best to guide us. May God bless you."

The Prophet said, "Do you swear to the worship of the One God, to my Divine mission and to the truth of the day of the Resurrection when the dead shall be raised on that day?" Everyone answered, "Yes. We so swear." He said, "May God be my witness..."

Then he said, "O people! Do you hear me?" They said, "Yea," and following that, every one was silent and other than the sound of the breeze, nothing could be heard. The Holy Prophet then said, "Now say what you will do with these two valuable things which I leave behind."

A person from among the multitude cried out, "What two valuable things?"

The Holy Prophet said, "First, the Book of the Holy Qur'an and do not remove yourselves from it so that you be led astray. The second valuable souvenir which I leave among you is my family. God the Almighty has informed me that these two will never separate from each other; they will join me in heaven and you will be destroyed if you part from these two. If you remain behind, again, you will be destroyed."

The Holy Prophet looked around him. He was looking for someone. Then he saw 'Ali. He bent down and took his hand and pulled him up so that the whiteness under the arms of both showed and all of the people saw him and recognized him.

Here the voice of the Holy Prophet became louder and clearer. He said, "What person from among all people is the most worthy of the believers?"

They answered, "God and the Prophet know best."

Then he said, "God is my Master and Leader and I am the master and leader of the believers and I am most worthy among them." Then he added, "Whoever I am the master and leader of, 'Ali is his master and leader." He repeated this three times and according to some Traditions, four times. Then he raised his head to the heavens and said, "God loves his friends, and hates those who hate him. Befriend his friends and leave those who do not befriend him. Know that his is in the right and that he follows the right."

Then he said, "All of those present, tell all of those who are absent." The people were still gathered when Gabriel, the trustee of God's message appeared and revealed verse 58 of surah 5 to the Holy Prophet. Then the Holy Prophet said, "I praise God. I praise God because he has completed his message and his blessings have ended for me and His satisfaction with my message and the wilayat of 'Ali has been announced after me."

A great commotion appeared among the people and then they congratulated 'Ali for the station he had been given. Abu Bakr, Umar, in the presence of the crowd said to 'Ali, "Congratulations to you, O son of Abu Talib, you have become my leader and leader of all of the people, men and women who have faith."

The above Tradition has been recorded in varying versions, some quite lengthy and some short, by many of the scholars of Islam in their books. This Tradition is greater than for one to deny or doubt that the Prophet said it. The scholar, Allamah Amini, in his famous book al-Ghadir mentions 110 people among the Companions and followers of the Prophet and 360 famous books on Islam in which it has been recorded and it has appeared in many of the books of the Sunni brothers on Traditions.

Lesson 36

Even a large group of the scholars of Islam have written independently about this Tradition, including Allamah Amini who himself has written an excellent, independent book about the particularities of this Tradition. The names of 26 Islamic scholars have been included in a separate book.

A number of the people who have seen this Tradition as being something which cannot be denied, have tried to deny it in discussing the issue of imamate and caliphate and have said that the word mula' (master) here means friend whereas if one notes the Tradition with care, the conditions under which it was recorded and the place where it was recorded, it is clear that the intention behind it was none other than imamate and wilayat in the sense of leadership of the people:

1.The verse on endeavoring to have Islam be better understood, which we have presented in the previous discussions, and before this, the situation in which it descended with the strong tone of recitation which appeared in it, well shows that the words are not about friendship and normal or average honesty because the was no place for such concern and all of this importance and emphasis was not necessary.

Also the verse of *Ikmal ad-Din* which was revealed after that shows that the above issue was extremely important like the issue of leadership and the successor to the Prophet which was relevant.

2. The method in which the Tradition was stated with all of the introductory remarks in the burning wilderness, with the extensive sermon, having the people swear to their beliefs and in a sensitive time and place are all proof of our claim.

3. The congratulations which the various groups of people gave to 'Ali and the poems that poets recited that day and on the following days, all are proof of this expression that the words are about the selection of Hazrat 'Ali to the position of imamate and wilayat and nothing else.

Think and Answer

1. Describe the story of Ghadir.

2. Narrate the Tradition of Ghadir with several proofs which have been mentioned about the Prophet in several famous books on Islam.

3. Why does the word *mula* in the Tradition of Ghadir refer to imamate and leadership and not friend?

Lesson 36

4. What prayer did the Holy Prophet recite and what were the events of Ghadir concerning the rights of 'Ali?

5. Where are Ghadir and Jahfah?

Lesson 37: The Tradition of Manzalah and the Tradition of Yawm Ad-Dar

Many of the great Shi'ite and Sunni commentators upon the Holy Qur'an say in commenting upon 7:142 that it refers to Moses, peace be upon him, leaving for 40 days to go to the place of the covenant and the selection of Aaron to succeed him, which have been recorded in the famous Tradition of *manzalah*.

The Tradition states when the Prophet was moving towards the battlefield of Tabuk (Tabuk was a place in the north of the Arabian peninsula which shared a border with the Eastern Roman Empire), he left 'Ali in his place in Medina.

They informed the Holy Prophet that the Emperor of the Eastern Roman Empire had sent a great army to attack the Hijaz and Medina and Mecca so that they could kill the bud of the Islamic Revolution before its special human program and ideals of longing for the truth could be exported to its area.

'Ali said, "Do you leave me among the women and children, not allowing me to go to the battle of jihad and seek honor there?"

Lesson 37

The Holy Prophet said, "Are you not satisfied to be to me as Aaron was to Moses except that there will be no Prophet after me?"

These words can be found in the most famous books on the Traditions as recorded by the Sunnis, that is, namely, *Sahih Bukhari* and *Sahih Muslim* with the difference that in the former, all of the Tradition has been recorded and in the latter, all of the Tradition appears once and then in another place only the sentence, "Are you not satisfied to be with me as Aaron was to Moses except that there will be no Prophet after me?" appears by itself.

This has been recorded in many of the books of the sunnis, including the *Sunan ibn Majah, Sunan Thirmidi, Musnad Ahmad* and many others. The Companions who have recorded it are more than 20 people, among whom are Jabir ibn Abdallah Ansari, Abu Sa'd Khadani, Abdallah ibn Mas'ud and Mu'awiyah.

Abu Bakr Baghdad in the *History of Baghdad* records from 'Umar ibn Khattab, the following,

"He saw a man who was speaking in an unworthy manner to 'Ali. 'Umar said, "I think you are a hypocrite because I have heard that the Prophet said,

"'Ali is in relation to me as Aaron was to Moses, other than that after me there will be no Prophet.'"

It is notable that from the respected source of the Traditions, it can be seen that the Prophet of Islam did not only use this sentence on the occasion of the Battle of Tabuk but that he repeated it seven times on various occasions which shows its generality of meaning:

On the day when the covenant of brotherhood (*al-mawakhat awwal Mecca*) was made among the brothers in Mecca, the Prophet chose 'Ali as his brother and repeated this same sentence.

On the second day of *al-Mawakhat*, when the day of brotherhood between the Emigrants and the Helpers was repeated, this was repeated and the Prophet once again repeated the Tradition of *Manzalah*.

On that day when the Holy Prophet ordered that the doors which opened from the homes onto the mosque should be closed and he only allowed 'Ali's door to remain open, he repeated this same sentence.

Thus it was stated on the occasion of the battle of Tabuk and three other times, the documentation of which is found in the books of Sunnis scholars. There is, then, no room for doubt neither from the point of view of documentation nor from the point of view of the generality of the meaning.

The Content of the Tradition of Manzalah

If we study the above Tradition, and we put aside any pre-judgments, we can make use of this Tradition to show that all of the positions which Aaron had among the Bani Israel in respect to Moses, 'Ali had except as to the Prophet because no other conditions exist in the Tradition.

Thus, we can conclude that:

1. 'Ali was the choice of the ummah after the Prophet (as Aaron had such a position).

2. 'Ali was the minister and consultant or special assistant to the Prophet and a partner in his leadership because the Qur'an has proven this for Aaron (see 20:29-32).

3. 'Ali was the successor to the Prophet and as long as he was present, no one else could take this position, as Aaron had this in relation to Moses.

The Tradition of Yawm Ad-Dar

According to that which has appeared in Islamic history, the Prophet in 3 AH was assigned to make open his invitation which he had kept secret until then. As the Holy Qur'an says:

"*And admonish your nearest kinsmen.*" *(26:214)*

The Holy Prophet called his close family to the home of his uncle, Abu Talib. After they had eaten, he said, "O sons of Abdul Muttalib, I swear that I know no one among the Arabs who has brought anything better than what I have brought. I have brought the goodness of this world and the next and God has ordered me to invite you to these precepts and I will befriend one of you to be my brother and my successor."

No one showed any interest in his proposal, other than 'Ali, peace be upon him, who was the youngest among them. He arose and said, "O Prophet of God, I am your helper upon this way." The Prophet put his arm around his neck and said, "This brother is my inheritor and my successor among you. Listen to his words and obey his orders."

But the lost tribe did not accept and turned to magic.

The above famous Tradition is called Yawm ad-Dar (the day of the invitation in the home). It is clear proof that many of the Sunnis scholars like ibn Abi Jarir, ibn Abi Hatam ibn Mardawiyah, Abu Na'im,

Biliaqi, Thalibi,Tabari, ibn Athir, Abu al-Fada and others have recorded it (for further information see al-Marajiat, p. 130 and Kitab al-Haqaqah al-Haqq, vol. 4, p. 62).

Whenever we study this Tradition, without any prejudgments, the truth of 'Ali's caliphate and wilayat becomes clearer to us because it refers directly to caliphate and leadership.

Think and Answer

1. What is the Tradition of Manzalah? How many People have confirmed it?

2. What was the content of the Tradition of Manzalah and what position did it prove for 'Ali?

3. Aaron had what position in relation to Moses, according to the Holy Qur'an?

4. Which scholars have recorded the Tradition of Manzalah?

5. What does the Tradition of Yawm ad-Dar and its content and documentation show?

Lesson 38: The Tradition of Thaqalayn and Noah"s Ark

The Documentation of the Tradition of Thaqalayn

One of the famous Traditions among the 'ulama of the Sunnis and Shi'ites is the Tradition of Thaqalayn.

A large group of the Companions, without any break, recorded this Tradition from the Prophet and some of the great 'ulama say that 30 of the Companions have mentioned it (*Sirah Halabi*, vol. 33, p. 308)

A large group of the recorders have mentioned this in their books and there can be no doubt as to this Tradition.

The great scholar, Sayyid Hashim Bahrani, in his book, *Ghayat al-Maram*, mentions this Tradition with 39 documentations from the Sunni scholars and 80 documentations from the Shi'ite 'ulama. Mir Hamad Husayn Hindi, another great scholar who studied this issue further, mentioned 200 Sunnis who have recorded this Tradition and he has compiled them in 6 volumes.

Among the individuals of the famous Companions who have recorded this are Abu Sa'id Khudari, Abu

Lesson 38

Dharr Ghifari, Zayd ibn Arqam, Zayd ibn Thabit, Abu Rafa', Jabir ibn Matam, Huzaifah, Damarah Islami, Jabir ibn Abdallah Ansari and Umm Salimah.

The basic Tradition, according to Abu Dharr Ghifari, is that once when he was in the Ka'bah, he turned to the people and said that I heard that the Holy Prophet had said "I leave two things of value among you: the Qur'an and my family. These two will never separate from each other until they enter unto me in the Fountain of Abundance (kawthar) in Paradise. Thus, take care to follow what I have recommended." (Recorded from *Jama' Tarmjghi as from Niyabi'al-mawadah*, p. 37).

This Tradition is found in the most reliable of the Sunni sources such as *Sahih Tarmidhi Nisai Musnad Ahmad Kanz al-Amal and mustadrak Hakirn*, etc.

In many of the books, this Tradition has been called Thaqalayn (two valuable things) and in some it is called *khalifitin* or two successors which do not differ in meaning.

It is interesting to note that in the various Traditions of Islam, this verse has been used by the prophet for the people on different occasions.

In the Tradition of Jabir ibn Abdallah Ansari, we read that he said this on the hajj on the day of Arafah.

It is recorded in a Tradition of Abdallah ibn Khattab that in Juhfah (an area between Mecca and Medina where some of the pilgrims enter the state of ihram).

It is recorded in a Tradition of Umm Salimah where this is said at Ghadir Khum.

It is recorded in a part of the Tradition during the last days of his blessed life, while he was on his death bed.

It is recorded in a Tradition he said this upon the pulpit in Medina (*al-Marajat*, p. 42)

Even famous Sunni scholars mentioned it ibn Hajar in his book, *Sawaiq al-Mahraqah* says from the Holy Prophet, "The Holy Prophet of Islam, after saying this Tradition, took 'Ali's hand and pulled him up and said, "It is 'Ali and the Qur'an and the Qur'an and 'Ali. They will not separate from each other until they enter unto me in the Fountain of Abundance" (*al-Sawa'jn al- Mahraqah*, p.75)

In this way, it becomes clear that the Prophet has expressed this as a principle many times and emphasized this and that he made use of many opportunities to express it so that it would never be forgotten.

The Content of the Tradition of Thaqalayn
Here, several points should be noted:

1. The introduction to the Qur'an and his family as 'two caliphs' or 'two valuable things' is clear proof that Muslims must never turn away from these two, especially with the condition in many Traditions where it states that, "If these two are released or freed from each other, you will be lost."

2. Placing Qur'an beside his family and his family beside Qur'an is proof that as the Holy Qur'an will never be altered and that it will be preserved, the family of the Holy Prophet had the position of infallibility.

3. In some of these Traditions, it has been stated that the Prophet said, "On the Day of Resurrection, I will question you about how you behaved towards these two great souvenirs, to see how you have acted towards them."

4. No matter how we interpret the Ahlul Bayt, 'Ali is the best confirmation. According to the

repeated Traditions, he will never be separated from the Holy Qur'an nor Qur'an from him.

In addition to this, in the repeated Traditions, we read that when the verse was revealed about *mubahilah*, the Holy Prophet called 'Ali, Fatimah, Hasan and Husayn, peace be upon them, and said, "This is my Ahlul Bayt.' (*Mash kat al -Masbaih*, p. 568, printed in Delhi and *Riyadh al- Nafarah*, Vol. 2, p. 248, recorded from Muslim and Tarmidhi).

1.Even though it is not clear to us who are enclosed in this world what will be questioned of us, but on the Day of Judgment, we know from the Traditions, that the meaning of the Fountain of Abundance which is a special stream in Paradise with many special privileges is for the real believers, the prophets and the Ahlul Bayt and the followers of that school.

From what has been said, it becomes clear that the leadership of the ummah of Muslims after the Prophet is through 'Ali and after him, also, through the Imams from this family.

Lesson 38

The Tradition of Noah"s Ark

An interesting statement is recorded from the Holy Prophet, in both Sunni and Shi'ite books on Traditions, which is the famous Tradition of Noah's ark.

In this Tradition, Abu Dharr says, "The Prophet said, "My family is like Noah's ark. Whoever uses it will be saved and whoever separates from it will drown."" (*Mustadrak Halcam*, vol.3, p. 151).

This Tradition, which is also among the famous Traditions and mentions the necessity for the people to follow 'Ali and the family of the Prophet after his death, has been emphasized.

Noting that the ark of Noah is a place of refuge and a means of salvation for when the great storm comes, this truth becomes clear that the Islamic ummah will be saved in the storm which came after the death of the Prophet through the Ahlul Bayt.

Think and Answer
1. What does the Tradition of Thaqalayn say and what benefits does it prove for the Ahlul Bayt?

2. Who recorded the Tradition of Thaqalayn?

3. What does Thaqalayn mean? And can other interpretations be given about its meaning?

4. In what situation did the Prophet say it?

5. Describe the Tradition of Noah's Ark from the point of view of its content and documentation.

Lesson 39: The Twelve Imams

The Traditions on the Twelve Imams

After proving imamate and the caliphate of Imam 'Ali, peace be upon him, we will mention the Traditions in relation to the other Imams.

There are repeated Traditions in the Sunni and Shi'ite books in our hands today which speak about caliphate of the twelve imams and caliphs after the Holy Prophet.

These can be found in many of the famous Traditions of the Sunnis, like *Sahih Bukhari, Sahih Tarmadi, Muslim Sahih Abu Dawoud and Musnad Ahmad*.

In the book *Muntakhib al-A thar*, there are 271 Traditions in this area which have been recorded and a large part of them are from Sunni scholars.

As an example, the *Sahih Bukhari*, the most famous book of the Sunnis says, "Jabir ibn Samarah says, "I heard the Prophet say, "There will be twelve leaders after me."

Then he said, "I heard that my father said he heard Prophet say, "They will be from the Quraysh.." (*Bukhari*, part 9, *Kitab al-Maqadam*, p. 100).

In *Sahih Muslim*, this same Tradition has been recorded in this way that Jabir says, "I heard the Prophet Say "Islam will always be dear until twelve caliphs and successors." Then he said something which I did not understand.

I asked my father and he said, "The Prophet said, "They are all from the Quraysh." (*Sahih Muslim, Kitab al-amanah, bab al-mal tih '1-quraysh*).

In *Musnad Ahmad* it has been recorded from Abdallah ibn Mas'ud, a famous companion, that he asked the Prophet about his vicegerents. He said, "They are twelve people like the Israeli tribes who were twelve people."(*Musnad Ahmad*, vol. 1, p. 398).

The Meaning of this Tradition

In some books of the Traditions, the power of Islam is referred to as being a pawn in the twelve caliphs and in others, the survival and life of religion are in the hands of a group of them until the Day of Resurrection and all are from the Quraysh.

In some, all of them are mentioned as being of the Bani Hashim. However it be, this Tradition does not conform to any sect except the Shi'ite because its explanation is very clear according to Shi'ism where the ulama of the Sunnis are at an impasse trying to explain it.

Lesson 39

Does it refer to the first four caliphs and then the Umayyid and Abbasid caliphs?

Whereas we know that the number of the first caliphs were twelve, but they did not end with the Umayyids or the Abbasids and the number twelve does not conform to anything.

In addition, among the Umayyid there are people like Yazid and among the Abbasids, people like Mansur Dawaniq, Harun al-Rashid, the oppression, arrogance and crimes of whom no one can deny and it is not possible that they be considered to be the caliphs of the Prophet and among the honor of Islam. No matter how much we simplify the criteria, they clearly do not include them.

And beyond these, the number twelve only can apply to the Shi'ites.

It is better that we now turn to a famous scholar, Sulayman ibn Abraham Qaduzi Hanafi in Yanabi'a al-Muwa-dat.

"Some of the scholars have said that, "The Tradition which mentions the rule of the caliphs after the Prophet are twelve people is famous and it has been recorded in many places.""

That which we can surmise is that, after the passing of time, what the Prophet of God was referring to was twelve successors from the *Ahlul Bayt* and his family because it is not possible that this Tradition refer to the first caliphs because they are only four people and it does not conform to the Umayyids because they were more than twelve people and all of them, other than Amr ibn Abdal Aziz were oppressors and also, they were not from the Bani Hashim and the Holy Prophet said, "All twelve are from the Bani Hashim."

When Abdal Malik ibn Umar records from Jabir ibn Sahrah and how the Prophet quietly said who they were from, he bore witness to what he said because some people were not happy about the caliphate of the Bani Hashim and the Tradition does not conform to the Bani Abbas, either, because they were more than twelve people and beyond this, they did not conform to the verse:

"No reward do I ask of you except the love of those near of kin... "(42:23)

Thus, the Tradition only can relate to the twelve Imams of the *Ahlul Bayt* and the family of the Prophet.

It refers to those whose knowledge is higher than that of any others, whose piety is unquestioned and from all points of view, are more knowledgeable and who gained their knowledge from the Prophet of Islam.

That which confirms this view is the Tradition of Thaqalayn and many other Traditions which have come from the Prophet. (*Yanabi 'al -Muwadat*, p. 446).

It is interesting to note another commentary upon this Tradition, "Perhaps by twelve caliphs and Amirs it is the first four, who existed at the beginning of Islam and the other eight have not appeared yet but will come in the future!"

In this way, it denies the relation and unity of the caliphs mentioned in the Tradition of the Prophet which is so clear.

But what we wish to say is that what is the necessity for commentary upon a Tradition which is so clear and conforms to the twelve Shi'ite imams and instead cause oneself to fall into these pits and crevices?

The Imams by Name

It should be noted that in some of the Traditions which have reached us from the Sunnis, the names of the twelve Imams have clearly appeared and their names specified!

Shaykh Sulayman Qanduzi, a famous Sunni scholar, in the book, *Yanabi' al-Muwarjdah* says,

"A Jewish man named Na'thal, went to the Prophet and among the questions he asked who would succeed him. The Prophet said, specifying them, "After me, 'Ali ibn Abi Tahib and then my two Sons, Hasan and Husayn and after Husayn, nine Imams will follow from his children."

The Jewish man said, "Name them.'

The Prophet said, "When Husayn leaves this world, his son, 'Ali, and after him, his child Muhammad and after Muhammad his son Ja'far and after Ja'far, his son Musa and after Musa, his son 'Ali and after 'Ali, Muhammad. After Muhammad, his child, 'Ali and after 'Ali, Hasan and after Hasan, his child Muhammad al-Mahdi. These are the twelve Imams." (*Yanabi 'al- Muwadat*, p. 431).

In that same book another Tradition is quoted from *Kitab Manaqib* with their titles and it indicates that

Imam Mahdi is in occultation and then he will arise and replace the oppression and tyranny which exists upon the earth with justice." (*Yanabi al-Muwadat*, p.442).

Of course, there are many Traditions relating to this in Sunni sources. (Note this with care).

Whoever dies and does not know his Imam of Time."

It is interesting to note that in the Sunni books, it is recorded from the Prophet, "A person who dies not knowing the Imam of his Time is as a man who lived in the Age of Ignorance." (*al- Majim al-Mufrist*, vol. 6, p. 302).

This same Tradition in Shi'ite sources says, "A person who dies and does not recognize the Imam of his, dies in a time of ignorance." (*Sajad al-Aswar*, vol. 6, p. 16).

These Traditions clearly show that a pure Imam lives in every age who must be recognized and whosoever does not do so, it is as if he had lived in an age of kufr and ignorance.

Is the Imam referred to in this Tradition that same person who rules the people? Ghengis', Haruns and dependent leaders?

Doubtlessly, the answer is negative because many the leaders are corrupt and oppressors sometimes act according to the East or the West and depend on the orders of foreign governments and they will clearly be sent to hell.

Thus it becomes clear that in every age and period there is an infallible Imam who must be found and recognized.

Of course, proof of the imamate of each Imam and the Traditions of each Imam who would follow, all exists.

Think and Answer

1. What books have recorded the twelve Imams?

2. What do these Traditions say?

3. What unacceptable explanations have been given about these Traditions?

4. Have the names of the twelve Imams appeared in Sunni sources?

5. What other way exists to prove the twelve Imams?

Lesson 40: The Twelfth Imam, The Great Leader and Peace-Maker of the World

The End of the Night of Darkness

When we look at our present situation, and we see the increase in crimes, massacres, wars, bloodshed, conflicts, international differences and the daily increase in corruption, we ask ourselves if the situation will continue in the same way and the extent of the crimes and corruption will so grow that all of society will be included in a continuous war and destroyed?

Or the ideological differences and ethical corruption will, like quicksand, take society along with it or is there still hope that one day humanity will be saved and reformed?

There are two answers to this important question.

The first answer: This is mentioned by the materialists and the pessimists and that is that the future of the world is dark and that every moment, a danger exists.

The second is of those who believe in the divinely revealed religions, in particular, the Muslims and, especially the Shi'ites, who give another answer to this question and they say: Behind this dark night lies the morning of hope.

These dark, stormy, death-like clouds and the flood of destruction will finally be eliminated and the clear heavens and the brilliant sun and a quiet environment will follow.

These hidden hurricanes will not always be before us and in the near future, we will be taken to the shore of salvation.

The world is in anticipation of a great Reviver who will, through a revolution, transform the world to the advantage of truth and justice.

Of course, we must note that each religion calls this leader by a different name. As an Arab poet says, "We call you by different names. But your beauty is not more than one thing and all of our words are directed towards that world of beauty!"

The Primordiality and Manifestation of this Great Reviver

Our inner inspirations whose waves come through the judgment of wisdom are more powerful, not only in the issue of ontology, which can guide us in all of our religious beliefs, but also guides us in this issue.

Lesson 40

Its signs:

First, the general love for justice of the world because all of the people of the world, in spite of all of the differences which they have, without exception, show love for peace and justice. We all cry out and make endeavors upon this way and we seek peace and justice of the world with all of our being.

A more important reason than this for the primordiality of the manifestation of a great Reviver cannot be found because the generality of such a need is proof of its Primordiality (Note this with care).

Every love and primordiality speaks of the rule of existence of a beloved and is moving to attract it.

How is it possible that God place this thirst in the inner spirit of the human being and not provide a fountain which will quench this thirst?

It is here that we say that the primordiality and nature of the seeking of justice of human beings cries out.

One day justice and peace will take over the entire world. The organizations of oppression will be destroyed. Humanity will take on the form of one country and will live under One flag, with solidarity and Unity and Purity of life. Another sign is the commonality which exists in all religions of the world as to the existence of a great Reviver.

In more or less all of the religions, such a chapter exists and the idea of the belief in the manifestation of a savior of the people who will heal all of the wounds of humanity is not only present among Muslims but rather all of the documents show that this is a universal belief which is primordial and exists in all of the religious groups of the East and the West, even though Islam, which is a more complete religion, places greater emphasis upon it.

Intellectual Proof

The order of the creation is a lesson for us that the world of humanity must, in the end, be ruled by the law of justice and remains based on a system of justice and peace.

This means that the world of existence, to the point that we know, is a complex of orders, systems and laws which are proof of the unity of the world and the connection to this system.

Lesson 40

The issue of order and law and programming and accounting is one of the most serious and basic issues of this world.

From the Milky Way to a minute atom, several million of which can be placed upon the head of a pin, all are of a special order.

The various organs of our body, from the amazing structure of a cell to the system of nerves and veins to the brain and the heart and the lungs, all have a particular order which is such that some scholars say that each one is like a clock which works within the body and the greatest computers are nothing in comparison to it.

In such a world, can a human being exist as a part of this universal as an non-conformed and disorderly part with wars and bloodshed and oppression?

Does injustice and the real corruption of a society, a type of disorder, always rule over humanity?

The result is that the witnessing of the world of existence makes us aware of the fact that the end of human society is justice and order and that it will return to the man line of creation.

The evolutionary or transformative line of society is another proof for the future which is clear of the world of humanity because we can never deny this truth that human society, from the day that it recognized itself, has never stopped at one stage and is continuously moving forward.

From the material point of view, from the view of clothes, housing, type of food and means of transportation humanity has lived through the most basic of situations and today it has reached the stage which surprises the sight and intellect and most certainly this ascent will continue.

From the point of view of knowledge and culture, also, the direction is always one of ascent or increase and every day new discoveries and new information is gained.

This law of transformation or evolution will include spiritual, ethical and social aspects as well as humanness and will move towards a just law, permanent peace, justice and moral and spiritual virtues and if we see that today, moral corruption is increasing, this is also an area to prepare for a transformative revolution.

We can never say that corruption should be encouraged but we say that when corruption reaches beyond a certain point, it will bring about the reaction of a moral revolution. When human beings find themselves before a dead end as a result of their undesirable sins, their heads hit a stone wall, and their lives are near ending, they will at least, be prepared to accept such a principle that comes on behalf of a divinely inspired leader.

The Qur'an and the Manifestation of the Mahdi

In the great heavenly book, there are multiple verses which give the glad tidings of a great manifestation. We will only select one verse from among all of them to show this truth.

"God has promised, to those among you who believe and work righteous deeds, that He will, of a surety, grant them in the land, inheritance (of power) as He granted it to those before them; that He will establish in authority their religion — the one which He has chosen for them; and that He will change (their state), after the fear in which they (lived), to one of security and peace. They will worship Me (alone) and not associate aught with Me. If they do reject faith after this, they are rebellious and wicked" (24:55)

This verse well shows that finally the rule on the earth will be free of tyranny and oppressors and the righteous believers will rule over the universe.

Imam 'Ali ibn "Husayn, in commentating upon this verse, said, "This group, I swear by God, is those very followers of our school. God, by means of a man from our family will realize this promise and he is the Mahdi of this ummah.

Imam al-Mahdi in the Traditions

The Traditions about the world rule and its realization along with peace and justice, by means of an individual of the family of the Holy Prophet who is called the Mahdi, is so great in the Sunni and Shi'ite source books that they are beyond counting.

And Traditions in relation to the twelfth Imam and the successor to the Holy Prophet, and the ninth child of Imam Husayn and the immediate child of Imam Hasan Askari is also extensive in Shi'ite resources.

In the first part, that is, the extent of the Traditions about the appearance of the Mahdi from Sunni resources, it is sufficient that the Sunni scholars, in their books, directly recall it. In a publication from the Rabitah al-'Alim Islami, the greatest center of learning in the hijaz, it says,

"He is the twelfth orthodox caliph which the Holy Prophet mentioned in the Traditions of sahabah and these Traditions of the Mahdi have been recorded by

Lesson 40

many of the Companions of the Holy Prophet of Islam."

Then, after naming the 20 Companions of the Prophet who have recorded the traditions of the Mahdi, it continues, "Other than them, there is a large group who have recorded these Traditions... some of the Sunni scholars, have written books on the appearance of the Mahdi among Whom are Abu Na'im Isfahani, ibn Hujar Haitha, Shu Kani and Idris Maghrabi, Abu Abbas ibn Abdallah Mu'min." Then it adds, "A large group of the past and today of the Sunnis directly have accepted the succession of the Traditions of the Mahdi.

Then after mentioning the name of a group of them, it ends with these words, "A large number of commentators and memorizers have directly said that the Traditions of Mahdi are directly, clearly and decisively successive and the belief in the appearance of the Mahdi is obligatory.

This is among the clear beliefs of the Sunnis and none but the ignorant and heretics will deny it.

But as to Shi'ite Traditions

It is sufficient for us to know that hundreds of Traditions of the Prophet and the Imams have been recorded in this area so that it is beyond succession.

Among the Shi'ites, it is considered to be obligatory and no individual can be among the religious people and be unaware of it and not accept the appearance of the Mahdi, his particularities, his type of rule and his program. The great Shi'ite "ulama, from the beginning until today, have written many books in this area and they have gathered Traditions in this area.

As an example, we will present two or three Traditions and those who are interested in further study should read *Mahdi, Inqilabi Bozorg, Nuvid Imam* and *Imam* and the translation of the book al-Mahdi written by Sayyid Sadr al-din Sadr.

The Holy Prophet of Islam said, "If only one day remains from the life of this world, God will lengthen it so that the Mahdi will be sent from God to fill the earth, which is filled with tyranny and oppression, with justice and equity."

In a Tradition of Imam Sadiq, we read, "When the time of the arising of the rule of the Redeemer comes, he will establish it upon justice. Tyranny and oppression during his rule will be eliminated; roads and passage ways during his rule, will be safe and the earth will be blessed.

Lesson 40

Every right will be given to its rightful owner and he, among the people, will judge like David and Muhammad. At this time, the earth will reveal its treasures and it will reveal its blessings. No needy person will be found because all believers will be without need.

Think and Answer

1. What is the difference between the thoughts of the believers and the materialists as to the future of the world?

2. Can one come to understand the manifestation of the Mahdi by means of primordiality? How?

3. Do we have intellectual proof for his appearance? Which proof?

4. What does the Qur'an say about this?

5. What does a study of the Traditions show?

Lesson 41: One Crucial Question: Is Death considered as One's End or Beginning?

Why Do Most People Fear Death?

Most people fear death. Why?

Death has always been imagined to be a great, frightening monster and just thinking about it takes away the sweetness of life.

Not only do they fear the word "death' but they also hate the word "cemetery' and they try to forget about its basic nature by lighting and brightening the graves and tombs.

The effects of this fear is clearly visible in the various literatures of the world where it is expressed as "the monster of death', "the jungle of death', "the death knoll', etc.

When they want to mention the name of a dead person, so that the person addressed not panic, they use sentences like "far from here', "may I be struck dumb', "there be seven mountains between', and "may his dust give you life' in an attempt to create a wall between the person who is listening and death.

But we have to analyze how this fear developed the human being.

Why is there a group, as opposed to the understanding of the majority of the people, who not only do not fear death but thinking about it makes them smile and welcome an honorable death?

We read in history that whereas one group were looking for the elixir of life, another group lovingly moved towards the fronts of jihad, laughed at the image of death and they were in

anticipation of the day when they would join their Beloved and today, also, in the battlefronts of truth against falsehood, we see this very truth whereby they move with their life in their hands, towards martyrdom.

The Basic Reason for this Fear With research and study we reach this point that the basis for this fear is simply one of two things:

The Interpretation of Death as Annihilation

Human beings always flee from non-existence and from disease because it means the lack of good health; are afraid of darkness because it means a lack of light. They fear poverty because it means the destruction of wealth.

They even sometimes fear an empty home and an empty wilderness. Why? Because nobody is there!

They even fear a dead person. They are not prepared to spend the night in a room with a dead person whereas when that person was alive, they did not fear him.

Now let us see why human beings fear non-existence and non-being. The reason is clear. Existence is woven into existence. Being is familiar with being. Being is never familiar with non-being. Thus, our alienation with non-being is completely natural.

If we believe and know that death is the end of everything and assume that with death, everything ends, have a right to fear it and even be terribly frightened by the mention of the word. Why? Because death will take everything from us.

But if we believe death to be the beginning of a new and eternal life, we will not have that fear; rather, we congratulate those who, with dignity and nobility, move wards it.

Lesson 41

Black Files

We all know of a group who do not interpret as being annihilation and non-being and they would deny life after death but in spite of this, they have great fear of death.

Why? Because the file of their deeds is so black they are afraid of the punishments after death; they have a right to fear death. They are like prisoners who fear the day they will be freed from prison because they know that when they are freed from prison, they will be executed.

He sticks to the prison bars, not that he is afraid freedom, he is afraid of the freedom whose result is punishment of execution. In this way, a person who does evil deeds, fears the freeing of his spirit from the ness of his body and knows this to be the beginning of his punishment and chastisement for his evil deeds and his oppression.

But those who neither see death to be annihilation nor do they have files of black deeds, why should they fear death?

They are also people who love being alive but to gain more benefits for their new life in a world after death for they welcome the death which comes upon the their goal which is well-pleasing to the Nourisher.

Two Different Points of View

We have said that people are of two kinds, one group of which forms the majority who fear and hate death.

But another group welcomes death if it is upon the way of their great goal like martyrdom upon the Way of God, or at least when they sense that their life is near the end, they never allow fear to enter their hearts. The reason is that they have two different points of view.

The first group: they either have absolutely no belief in life after death or if they believe in it, they have not really, as yet, accepted this belief, thus they believe the moment of death to be the moment to bid farewell to all things. Of course, to bid farewell to everything is most difficult; leaving the light and taking steps in the darkness of the absolute is most painful.

Also, being freed from a prison and going towards a trial for a criminal whose crimes are obvious is frightening and fearful.

But the second group believes death to be a new birth, moving beyond the limited and dark environment of this world, taking steps into an extensive world and one which is full of light.

Being freed from the narrow prison or cage of the body and flying in infinite space, leaving behind an environment in which the center of small mindedness, tensions, injustices evil opinions and wars and stepping into an environment which is cleansed of these corruptions. It is natural that they have no fear of such a death.

Just like Imam 'Ali, peace be upon him, he said, "I swear that 'Ali, the son of Abu Talib, looks forward to death with greater desire than a baby looks forward to its mother's breast."

It is not without reason that in the history of Islam, we encounter people like Imam Husayn and his faithful companions who, as the moment for their martyrdom comes, are overjoyed and they hurry towards their meeting with their Beloved.

And it is also for this reason that in the honorable life of Hadrat 'Ali, peace be upon him, we read that when the sword struck his head, he cried out, "I swear by the God of the Ka'bah that I have been relieved."

It is clear that the meaning of these words is not that a human being not appreciate the blessings of this world and overlook them, and not make use of them to attain great goals, but rather, what is meant is that in life, correct benefits be gained, but at the end, never allow room for fear, knowing that it is upon the way of great and sublime goals.

Think and Answer

1. Why do people fear death and what is the reason for it?

2. Why does one group smile at death and move unhesitatingly towards it with the love of martyrdom?

3. What can the moment of death be compared with? What feelings do those who are pure and good-doers have and what feelings do those have who are not?

4. Have you ever seen people who were not afraid of death? What memories of them do you have?

5. What was Hadrat 'Ali's logic about death?

Lesson 42: Belief in The Resurrection Gives Meaning to Life

If we take this world into consideration, without concerning ourselves with any other, it will be meaningless and empty.

It is similar to the time of life when a fetus is not in this world, but is in the womb.

A child who is within its mother's womb and who is imprisoned for months in this darkness and narrowness, if it was to have wisdom and intellect, and was to think about its being a fetus, it would be very surprised.

Why am I imprisoned in this dark prison?

Why do I have to move in water and blood?

What result will the end of my life have?

When did I come, why have I come?

But if one is made aware of the fact that this is a Preliminary stage, that their organs are formed here, they gain strength and become prepared for movement in this great world.

After the passing of 9 months, it is freed, it moves into a world in which the sun shines, the moon reflects, green trees and streams of water flow and multiple benefits are attained; then it takes a deep breath and says, "Now I have understood the philosophy of my existence here."

This is a preliminary stage; this is a place to fly from; this is a class to pass through in order to move towards a great university.

But if the life of a fetus is cut off from life in this world, everything will become dark and meaningless – a frightening prison with purposeless and harmful results.

This is exactly the point in the relation of life in this world with life after death.

What is the point in our living more or less 70 years in this world?

For a time, we are immature and inexperienced and by the time that we become mature, our life ends.

For a time, we must study and work and by the time that we study and learn, we have reached old age.

Why are we alive? To eat, wear clothes and sleep? And repeating this life day after day.

Lesson 42

Is this extensive universe, this expansive world and the storing of all of this knowledge and experience, all of these teachers and instructors, all repeated for eating, drinking and putting on clothes?

It is here that the meaninglessness of this life will be clear to those who do not believe in the next world because they cannot reckon this small issue to be the goal of life and they do not believe in the next world either.

Thus, it can be seen that a group of them try to commit suicide and end this absurd life. But if we believe that this world is a pasture for the after life or that it is a field which must be planted and

then be taken as eternal life, that the world is a university in which we must learn and prepare ourselves for life in an eternal world, and that the world is a bridge which we must cross over, in this case, the world will not appear to be absurd and futile Rather it will be the beginning for an eternal life and no matter what efforts we make towards it, are small.

Yes. Faith in the resurrection gives meaning to human life and frees a person from anxiety, worry and absurdity.

Faith in the Resurrection is an Important Factor in Training

In addition to this, belief in the existence of a Court of the Day of Judgment is most effective in our daily lives.

Assume that it were to be announced in a country that there will be no punishment for such and such a crime and no records will be kept, that people can, with a clear conscience, live the day as they so desire. They give the day off to the police, the army and security forces. They lock the doors of the courts and until the next day when life will begin as normal, no crimes will be punished.

How do you think that society will spend that day? Belief in the resurrection, faith in the Day of Judgment, is in no way comparable to this world.

The details of this Court are as follows:

1. It is a trial, in which explanations are ineffective, nor can relations rule over norms nor can false statements be presented to change the decision.

2. It is a court which does not need the facilities of this world and because of this, it is not extended to take more time; it is studied like lightening and a decision is given immediately.

3. It is a court in which the file or record of people is their own deeds, that is, their deeds will themselves be present and made known by their actions in such a way that there is no way to deny them.

4. The witnesses in that court are his or her hands and feet, eyes and ears, tongue and skin and even the earth and the walls of a house in which there was sin or good deeds were committed will be there, witnesses which are like the effects of nature and cannot be denied.

5. This court is one whose Judge is God Almighty, God Who is Aware of all things, is Needless of all and Who is more Knowing than all others.

6. Beyond this, the punishments there are not contractual; it is our acts themselves which take form and will be alongside us and they will punish us or draw us into blessings.

Faith in such a court takes a person to the point that Hadrat 'Ali says, "I swear to God that if I were to spend from night to the morning upon thorns and if my hands and feet were to be chained in the day and I were to be pulled through the streets and the bazaars, I am more willing to have this happen than to present myself to God's Court if I have committed an oppression against one of God's creatures or if I have usurped the rights of another." (Nahj al-Balaghah, Sermon 224)

Can a Person with such Faith be Deceived?

It is faith in this Judgment that makes a human being place his brother's hand near the fire to burn when he has extended it into the public treasury. And when the brother screams in pain, he advises him, "You are screaming from the flame of a toy fire which is in the hands of human beings whereas you take your brother to a fire which is extremely frightening and which is lit by the anger of the Creator?" (Nahj al-Balaghah, Sermon 224)

Can a person with such faith be deceived?

Can one buy his conscience with bribery?

Can he, with encouragement of threats, be made to deviate from the way of truth to the way of oppression?

The Holy Qur'an says when the scroll of deeds is shown to sinners, they cry out:

"Ah! Woe to us! What a book is this! It leaves out nothing small or great but takes account thereof!" (18:49)

In this way, powerful waves of the sense of responsibility grows towards the spirit of the human being which controls the human being from deviating, going astray, committing oppression and aggression.

Think and Answer

1. If there was nothing after this limited life and the situation of this world, what would happen?

2. Why does a group of those who deny the Resurrection deviate?

3. What are the differences between the Court of the Day of Judgment and the courts of this world?

4. What effects does faith in the Resurrection have upon the deeds of a human being?

5. What did Amir al-Mu'minin, 'Ali, peace be upon him, do to his brother Aqil? What did he want and what response did 'Ali give him?

Lesson 43: An Example of the Trial of the Day of Judgment is within You

Since the issue of the afterlife and the great court of the Resurrection would seem strange for someone who has lived inside the prison in this world, God has established a small court inside each one of us which is called the court of conscience.

To explain in more detail: A person will be tried in many courts for the crimes he has done the first court is the usual courts in this world with all its shortcomings.

Although the very presence of such courts would lessen the number of crimes, they are based on such feeble foundations that nobody expects them to act in complete accordance with justice.

If wrong laws are enforced in a court, if judges are busy taking bribes and are subject to nepotism and partisan influences, then we could not expect justice to prevail in such a court.

Even if some courts might be presided over by pious judges, there are still those clever criminals who could escape punishment.

The second type of court, which functions better than the first one, is the court of the consequences of our own deeds. Our acts have consequences which affect us sooner or later.

We have seen many governments that were engaged in tyranny and engaged in all forms of injustice, but were soon caught up in the traps they had made for themselves. They collapsed as a result of their wrong actions, caught in the consequences of what they had done earlier.

Such a court has the shortcoming that it is neither public nor universal. Therefore, it could not make us feel that we do not need the court of the resurrection.

The third court, which is more elaborate than the preceding one is the court of the conscience. In the same way that the solar system, with its wonderful system can be observed in the tiny structure of an atom, we could claim that the court of our conscience is a tiny example of the court of the resurrection.

This is because there is a mysterious force inside our inner self which is called "practical wisdom" by the philosophers, "the reproaching soul" by the Holy Qur'an and "conscience" by others.

As soon as man does a good or bad act, this court starts to operate immediately and issues its verdicts in the form of mental punishments or mental rewards.

This court of conscience at times beats the wrongdoer inside with such a force that he or she would prefer death to this life. Such a person would write in his will "if I commit suicide it was because I wanted to get rid of the tortures of my conscience."

This court of conscience at times encourages man for his good work to the extent that he becomes extremely delighted. He then feels at ease in his soul, and he could never find such a source of delight anywhere in the world.

Such a court has its own characteristics:

1. In this court, the judge, the witness, the officer to carry out the court's verdict, and the audience are the same person. It is the force of conscience that acts as a witness, that judges and finally carries out the verdict.

2. Contrary to normal judicial procedures which would sometimes take years to complete, the trial here at this court is momentary; it does not take time. Occasionally some time is needed to

remove the obscurities from the eyes of the beholder, however, as soon as the documents are in, the verdict will be issued.

3. The verdict of such a court does not require one to go to a court of appeal; it only has one stage.

4. This court will not only punish; it will also reward those who perform their duties. In such a court, both the good-doers and the wrongdoers are tried and receive rewards or punishment accordingly.

5. The punishment of such a court does not have anything in common with ordinary punishment in the sense that they do not require prisons, whips, or executions. However, at times they are so torturous for a person's soul that no punishment could compare to it. In sum, such a court does not resemble any worldly court; it rather resembles the court of the Resurrection. The greatness of the court of conscience is so tremendous that the Holy Qur'an swears by it, associating it with the court of the Resurrection:

"Nay! I swear by the Day of Resurrection. Nay! I swear by the self-accusing self. Does man think that we shall not gather his bones? Yea! We are able to make complete his very fingertips." (Qur'an 75:1-4)

Naturally, such a court, due to its material nature, does not make us feel that we do not need the court of the Resurrection. This is because:

1. The sphere of human conscience is not all-inclusive; rather, it is based on one's way of thinking.

2. At times, a treacherous man could deceive even his own conscience.

3. At times, the call of a wrongdoer's conscience is so weak that he cannot hear it.

Here, the significance of the fourth court, i.e., the court of the Resurrection will become clear.

Think and Answer

1. In reality in how many courts is a person tried?

2. What are the particularities of the first court and what is it called?

3. What particularities does the third court have?

4. What are the particular characteristics of the second court?

5. Describe the merits and weaknesses of the court of the conscience.

Lesson 44: Belief in Resurrection is Manifested in our Primordial Nature

We most often see that coming to know about God is within the primordiality and nature of a human being.

If we search into the awakened and non-awakened consciences of the human being, his faith and desire in a source which is metaphysical, we come upon a metaphysical source which is gained through knowledge, program and goal which created this world.

But this issue is not limited to monotheism and coming to know about God. All of the principles and practices which are basic to religion must be seen within this very primordial nature. Otherwise, the harmony which is necessary to exist between creation and the Divine Law will not be found. (Pay special attention here).

If we take a look at our heart and we discover the depths of the spirit and our soul, we hear these whisperings from the world that life does not end with death, but rather death is a window upon the world of survival.

In order to understand this truth, we must turn to the points below.

Love of Survival

If the human being has been created for annihilation and non-being, that person should desire non-being, and receive pleasure from death at the end of life whereas we see that this is not the case. Instead we see that death is in no time or era a pleasure and that many people flee from it with all of their being.

Looking for ways to lengthen one's life, looking for the Fountain of Youth, the Elixir of Life, the Water of Life are all signs of this truth.

This love for survival shows that the human being was created to survive and if we had been born for being and annihilation, this love would have no meaning.

All of the basic loves which are within our being are completed by it and the love for survival is a love which completes or perfects our being.

Note that we discuss the issue of the Resurrection after we have accepted the existence of God, the Wise, the Knower.

We believe that whatever He created in our bodies is based on a known measure and because of this, the love and desire of a human being for survival must also have an accounting and that can be nothing other than the existence of a world after this one.

Resurrection Among the Tribes of the Past

The history of humanity, as it bears witness, in a general sense, in the tribes of the past, from the earliest of times shows clear proof of the clear belief of the human being to life after death.

The traces which have remained from the human beings of the past, even those who existed before written records, in particular, the method of making graves for the dead and how they buried the dead, all bear witness to this truth that they believed in life after death.

This rooted belief which has always existed in humanity, cannot be believed to be a simple idea or only a habit.

Whenever a belief is found in the form of something which has roots, and throughout history, we see it in human society, we should know that it is part of primordial nature because it is only primordial nature which can persevere with the passage of time and social and intellectual changes and remain in its place. Otherwise, customs will be forgotten.

The wearing of a special type of clothes is either a question of habit or a form of custom, which, over time, either changes or is destroyed.

But the love of a mother for her child is instinctive. It is a part of nature and a symbol. Thus, with the passing of time, the flame of love does not decrease in various environments. Whatever efforts are made in this way are reasons why this is part of the primordial nature of a human being.

When scholars say that careful study has shown that the earliest of people had a kind of religious belief because they buried their dead in a special way and they placed their tools of work beside them, and in their own way and with their particular belief, they showed that they believe in the existence of another world.

We can then well see that they had accepted life after death, even if they were in error. They thought that life there was just like life in this world and that they would need those very same tools.

Lesson 44

The Existence of the Inner Trial

The existence of the inner trial or court called the Conscience is another reason for the resurrection being primordial.

Just as we have previously said, we all well sense that there is a trial or a court within us which judges what we do. It gives rewards for good deeds. We feel satisfied and our spirit overflows

with joy and happiness in such a way that the feeling is incapable of being described. In relation to evil deeds, and, in particular, great sins, they are felt in such a way that life becomes bitter.

It has often been seen that individuals, after committing a great crime, like murder and trying to escape from the scales of justice, voluntarily give themselves up. They surrender to the hangman's noose and the reason is the torture which the conscience gives.

A human being, on bearing witness to this trial or court, asks himself or herself, "How can I, who am but a small creature, have such a conscience but the great universe and the world of creation not have a trial or court which it is worthy of?"

In this way, we can prove that the belief in the resurrection and life after death is primordial in three ways:

1. Through love of survival.

2. Because of the existence of this belief throughout history.

3. Through a small example of that in our own selves.

Think and Answer

1. How can one distinguish that which is primordial from that which is not primordial?

2. What is the reason why a human being has a love for survival and what reason can this be for the primordiality of the resurrection?

3. Did the early people believe in the resurrection? Why?

4. How does the condemnation by our conscience encourage or punish us? Give examples of that.

5. What relation is there between the trial by one's conscience and the great Day of Judgment?

Lesson 45: The Resurrection & the Scales of Justice

A cursory look at the system of creation will reveal to us that everything is systematic and governed by rules.

In the body of man, this system is so delicate that any imbalance would lead to either sickness or death.

For instance, in the structure of the eyes, heart, and brain this order is readily noticeable. The same order, systematization, and justice prevail over all of creation.

Through justice, the skies and the earth have been erected.

An atom is so tiny that millions of them could be located in the point of a needle. Such an atom must be extremely precise and ordered in its structure to allow it to exist for millions of years.

This happens because of the justice and exact calculations that are employed in the construction of an atom.

Is man such an exceptional being as to be free to do what he pleases? Is he free? Or is there something hidden here?

Free will and Freedom in Decision-Making

One distinctive feature that distinguishes man from all other creatures is that he possesses freedom of action. Why has He created him free and given him the freedom of will to carry out what he wants?

The reason rests in the fact that if he were not free he would never develop. This freedom has ensured man's spiritual and ethical development.

Suppose one is forced at gunpoint to help and assist the needy and carry out those acts which are beneficial to the community. Even though his acts would be naturally useful to everyone no ethical or human perfection or maturity would have taken place.

Whereas, if he had carried out these actions voluntarily and he only did one hundredth of what he could have done, he still would have taken a big stride towards his perfection and development.

Thus, the first condition for spiritual and ethical perfection is to have a free will; man should do good things on his own and not through force. This great asset has been given to man just for this purpose.

Of course, this great asset is like a beautiful flower which is accompanied with thorns which represent the misuse of this free will.

Naturally, it would be quite easy for God to punish a man for his unjust deeds, to inflict him with all sorts of miseries, to make him blind, or dumb, or paralyzed altogether.

Under such circumstances, nobody would dare to do wrong things. But this abstention and piety then would be by force and could never be counted as a point of honor for man, for this piety would have been due to his fear of a great punishment.

Thus, man should be free. He should be exposed to God's different trials and not be threatened by immediate punishment so that he could show his true worth.

But there remains one issue to be solved. If each person could be free to do whatever he desires, this could negate God's Justice which governs the world.

That is why we become convinced that there should be a court for mankind in which everyone should be present and be tried to receive punishments if they had wronged others or given rewards if they have been just in their deeds.

Is it possible for Nimrods, Pharaohs, Genghis khans and korahs to commit atrocities carry out all sorts of unjust acts and then go away with no punishment whatsoever?

Could criminals and pious people be equal on God's scale of justice?

Regarding this, the Holy Qur'an says:

"What! Shall We then make those who submit as the guilty? What has happened to you? How do you judge?" (68:35-36)

and also:

"Shall We make those who guard against evil like the wicked?" (38:28)

It is a fact that some of the wrongdoers would be at least partially punished in this world for their devilish acts. It is also a fact that the court of conscience exists. It is also a fact that the consequences of one's unjust and devilish acts would inflict him later.

But if we consider the matter carefully, we will find out that no tyrant or sinner receives a punishment in this world proportional to the degree of his devilish acts. There are some who even escape the consequences of their wrongdoing.

So there should be a universal court in the other world to judge them justly and impartially or else the principle of justice would vanish forever.

Therefore, the acceptance of God and His system of Justice entails the acceptance of the Resurrection and the other world. These two are faces of the same coin.

Think and Answer

1. How is the heaven and the earth based upon justice?

2. Why has the human being been given free choice and will?

3. What would happen if a human being were to receive punishment immediately and directly for an evil deed in this world?

4. Why does the existence of the trial by conscience for our deeds not exempt us from the trial on the Day of Judgment?

5. What is the connection between the justice of the Creator and the Resurrection?

Lesson 46: We Have Seen the Resurrection Many Times in this World

The verses of the Holy Qur'an clearly show this truth that the idol-worshippers and also the other kufar, not only at the time of the Holy Prophet, but in other ages as well, were surprised or amazed by the issue of resurrection and life after death and they were frightened by it to the point that whoever mentioned it was considered to be insane and they would say to each other:

"The kuffar say (in ridicule), "Shall we point out to you a man that will tell you when you are scattered to Pieces in disintegration that you shall (then be raised) in a flew creation?"" (34:7)

Yes. In that age, because of a lack of knowledge and short-sightedness any mention of the belief in a life after death and a world after death was considered to be insanity or an insult to God and the belief that giving life to a dead body was considered to be insanity.

But it is interesting that opposed to this Way of thinking, the Holy Qur'an refers to various reasons of life which both a common average person can understand as well as scholars, each one to their own extent of ability Even though referring to all of the Qur'anic verses in this area requires a separate book, we have tried here to present some of them.

Sometimes the Qur'an says to them:

"It is God Who sends forth the winds so that they raise up the clouds and We drive them to a land that is dead and revive the earth therewith after its death; even so (will be) the Resurrection." (35:9)

We look at the visage of nature in the winter time.

Every place smells of death. The trees all lack leaves, fruit and blossoms and the only thing remaining of it is dry branches. Neither do the flowers laugh nor blossoms blossom nor is any movement of life to be seen.

The spring season arrives. The weather grows warmer, life-giving drops of rain fall. Suddenly a movement is seen in all of nature: flowers bloom, trees grow leaves, blossoms and flowers appear, birds find their places upon the branches of trees and it is glorious to see.

If life after death had no meaning, we would not see this scene every year before our eyes. If life after death was something which was absolutely impossible, and words of the insane, we would not be able to sense it every year before our eyes.

What difference is there between the life of the earth after death and the life of human beings after death?

Sometimes, the Qur'an also grips their hands and takes them to the beginning of creation and recalls it to them and refers to that Arab Bedouin who picks up a rotten bone and goes to the Prophet of Islam and says, "O Muhammad, who will be able to enliven this rotten bone? Tell me who?"

And he thinks that he has found the final proof for disproving the Resurrection. The Holy Qur'an says:

"Say, "He will give them life Who created them for the first time. For He is well-versed in every kind of creation!"
(36:79)

What is the difference between initiating creation and a new creation?

And the answer is found in another verse.

"Even as We produced the first creation shall We Produce a new one." (21:104)

Lesson 46

Sometimes the great Creation of God of the heavens and the earth is mentioned:

"Is not He Who created the heavens and the earth able to create the like thereof? Yea, indeed! For He is the Creator Supreme of skill and knowledge. Verily, when He intends a thing, His Command is, "Be," and it is." (36:81-82)

Those who doubted this issue were individuals who had short-sightedness and never saw beyond their own environment. Otherwise, they would know that a new creation or a recreation is easier than initiating of creation and the new life given by .God with all of His strength is not a difficult issue, and new creation is not a difficult task.

Sometimes the Resurrection energies have been mentioned whereby it says:

"The same Who produces for you fire out of the green tree, when behold! you kindle therewith (your Own fires)." (36:80)

When we study this wondrous verse of the holy Qur'an with care and we seek aid from today's science, science tells us that only green trees can store the energy of light of the sun and that when we burn a piece of wood and we make a fire, that is the same heat and energy which is similar to the heat of the sun which has been stored in it for years and we thought that that light and heat had died and had been destroyed but we see today that it has found new life.

For God Who has all of this power, who can store tens of years of the energy of light from the sun within a tree and in one moment bring all of it forward, and it receives new life, it is not a difficult task.

At any rate, we see with what logic and clarity the Holy Qur'an explains the issue of the resurrection to those who have doubts about it and they even thought that anyone who believed such a thing was insane. It clearly proves the existence of the resurrection, only a small part of which we have been able to mention here.

Think and Answer

1. Why are the multi-theists surprised by the issue of the Resurrection?

2. How is the Resurrection created each year for us in nature?

3. The Qur'an in a part of its verses shows that the life of a fetus is similar to the Resurrection Why?

4. What is the energy of the Resurrection?

5. Why has the Holy Qur'an emphasized the green tree?

Lesson 47: The Resurrection and The Philosophy of Creation

Many ask the question, "Why did God create us?"

And sometimes they go further than this and ask, "What is the philosophy of Creation of this great universe?"

A gardener plants a tree for its fruit and he plows the earth for seeds and spreads the seeds, why did the Great Gardner of Creation create us?

Was God lacking something that He created us?

If so, He will be in need of something and this does not suit the fact that He is in the station of the Creator and is Infinite in Existence.

There are many words which have been written in response to this question but it can be summarized in a few sentences.

It is a great mistake to compare God's Qualities with our own. As we are limited creature, everything we do is in order to eliminate a need. We study in order to make up for the deficiency we have in learning.

Lesson 47

We work in order to make up for the economic deficiency we have.

We seek after health centers and treatment in order to meet our health requirements.

In relation to God Who is Needless from all points of view, if we do something we must seek Him in other than His Existence. He does not create in order to benefit from His Creation, rather His goal is to Be for His creatures.

He is like a sun which is full of radiance and is Infinite without Him having any need, He illuminates so that all may gain advantage from it. This is what His Infinite Essence is and His special blessing where He has taken the hands of His creatures and moves them towards transformation and perfection.

Our creation from non-being was itself an outstanding step of transformation. The sending of the prophets and the descent of a heavenly Book and the formulation of laws and programs are each to be reckoned to be a basis for us.

"This universe is a great university and we are students in this university".

"This world is a readied pasture and we are the farmers of this land".

"This world is a beneficial, commercial center and we are merchants in this bazaar." (Nahj al- Balaghah)

How can we, for the creation of humanity, be the purpose of a goal? When we look around ourselves and we look at each and every creature, each one has a goal.

In the wondrous system or factory of our body, there is nothing which is without a goal including our eyelashes and the arches in our feet.

How is it possible that the structure of our body, each particle of it, have a goal but the totality of our being lack one?

We leave aside our own bodies and we look at the great world; we see that every system has a separate goal, the goal of the shining of the sun, the goal of rain falling, the goal of the special characteristics of the air that breathe, but it is possible that the totality of this then, lack a goal?

The truth is that within the heart of this expansive universe, it is as if these where a painting showing the final goal which we cannot always see at the first moment but it says, "Education and transformation."

Now that we have briefly become familiar with the goal of creation, words are about whether or not our life of a relative few days with all of its difficulties, problems and deficiencies can be the goal of creation?

Let us assume that I will live 60 years in this world and everyday from morning until night, I struggle to earn a living and at night, exhausted, I return home and the conclusion or result is that throughout my life, several tons of food and water are consumed and with difficulty, I purchase a house and then die and leave this world. Does this goal have the value to call me to live with all of these difficulties?

In truth, if an architect builds an enormous building in the wilderness and he spends many years completing it and he provides it with all of the necessary facilities and when he is asked, "What is your purpose?" He says, "My goal is that all of my life I build this building for passer-bys to spend an hour in it!

Will we not be surprised and will we not say, "Does one hour of rest of a passer-by need all of this effort?"

Because of this, those who do not believe in life after death, think that life in this world is absurd and this perspective is often repeated in the words of the materialists, to whom living in this world is purposeless. Often, among these individuals there are people who commit suicide because they are tired of this life.

That which gives purpose to life and makes it logical is because it is the preliminary for another life and the bearing of the difficulties of this life is preparatory for making use of the way towards an eternal life.

Here we had previously presented an interesting example, and that is that if a fetus which is in its mother's womb had sufficient intelligence and if they were to say to it, "There is nothing after this life for you," the fetus would most certainly object to this and would ask, "What purpose is there in my being imprisoned in this environment? To go through all this and then nothing?"

The Creator had a purpose in this creation!

But if we are assured that these several months are but a quickly passing phase and the preparatory stage for a relatively long life in this world, a world which in relation to the world of a fetus, is extensive and full of light and in relation to that it has several stages, the fetus will be assured that the period of gestation makes sense and that it has a goal and because of that, it is bearable.

The Holy Qur'an says:

"And you certainly know already the first form of creation. Why then do you not celebrate praises?" (56:62)

In summary, this world cries out with all of its being that there is another world after this world, otherwise it would be useless.

Listen to the words of the Holy Qur'an,

"Did you then think that We had created You in jest and that you would not be brought back to Ifs (for account)?" (23:115)

This refers to the fact that if there were no return to God, as mentioned in the Holy Qur'an, through the resurrection, the creation of human beings would be equivalent to being useless.

The conclusion is that the philosophy of creation says that after this world, another world must exist.

Think and Answer

1. Why can the Qualities of God not be compared to the qualities of a human being?

2. What was the purpose behind our creation?

3. Can life in this world be a goal for the creation of the human being?

4. A comparison of the life of a fetus with life in this world teaches us what?

5. What reasoning does the Holy Qur'an give for the creation of this world for the existence of the hereafter?

Lesson 48: The Survival of the Spirit, a Sign of the Resurrection

When the philosophers began to express the philosophy of humanity, they mentioned the spirit as being an important element in relation to other elements.

From then on, all philosophies presented a point of view about it to the point where some of the Islamic scholars have presented a thousand reasons for the truth of the presence of the spirit and issues relating to it. Much has been stated in this area but the most important issue which should be noted is that the answer to this question is:

Is the spirit material or not? And in other words, is it independent or not? Or does it have special chemical and physical properties like the brain and nerves?

Some of the materialist philosophers have said that the spirit and spiritual phenomena are both material and non-material and it is like the special cells of the brain and when the human being dies, the spirit disappears just like a watch which when broken, no longer works.

Alongside these philosophies are the philosophers of the divinely revealed traditions and even some of the materialist philosophers who believe in the originality of the spirit, believe that at the death of the body, the spirit does not die and continues to live.

In order to prove this, that is, the originality, independence and subsistence of the spirit, there are many complicated reasons. Here we will present some of the clearer ones in clear and simple terms.

A Great World Cannot be Placed Within a Small One

Assume that you are seated beside the sea and behind it are extremely high mountains. The roaring waves and the shaking of the water against the shore and with great strength, return to the sea.

We look at this scene for a moment. Then we close our eyes and see this scene in our minds with all of its greatness.

This shows that other than a body and cells of the brain, another jewel exists which can reflect any design no matter how great and at any scale. Clearly, this jewel must be something which is beyond the material world because we find nothing like it in the material world.

Lesson 48

The External Particularity of the Spirit
We have many chemical and physical properties in our bodies, the motion of the heart has a physical quality but the effects on food is a chemical substance and examples like this are many in our body.

If the spirit, thought and reflection were all material and had physical and chemical quantities of the brain cells then why among them and our other physical properties is there a great deal of difference?

Our thoughts, ideas and spirit relate and correct us to the external world and make us aware of that which passes outside but the chemical particularities of the stomach and the physical motion of our eyes and tongue and heart never has such a state.

Experienced Proof of the Originality and Independence of the Spirit
Fortunately, today scholars by various scientific and experimental means have proven the originality and independence of the spirit and permanently answered those who deny the truth of the independence of the spirit and all people who believe it to be material.

Hypnotism is among the clear reasons for this which the experiments have proven this.

We see dreams and scenes appear in our dreams which sometimes speak of the future and sometimes they clarify something which had been ambiguous in such a way that it cannot be called chance or accident which is a further proof for the independence of the spirit.

These examples show that the spirit is not material and that it is not the result of special physical or chemical properties of the human brain but rather it is a metaphysical truth which does not end when the body dies but, instead, prepares itself for the Day of Resurrection and the Hereafter.

Think and Answer

1. What is the difference of opinion between the Divine philosophers and the materialists as to the spirit?

2. What is the meaning of the non-conformity of something large with something small? Which is among the major reasons for the spirit?

3. How can truthful dreams be proof of the authenticity and independence of the spirit?

Lesson 49: The Physical-Spiritual Resurrection

Among the important questions which relates to the discussion of the Resurrection is, "Is the Resurrection only spiritual?" or does the body of an individual also appear in another world? and the human being take on the very form that he or she had in this world but in a higher and more elevated level? Continuing life in a new life?

Some of the ancient philosophers only believed in the spiritual Resurrection. They believed the body to be a composite, which is only with the human being in this world, and after death, becomes needless of that, and it is released and hurries towards the world of the spirit.

But in the view of the great Ulama of Islam, and many of the philosophers, is that Resurrection in both aspects, that is, spiritual and physical, takes place is correct that this body becomes dust and this dust spreads itself over the earth and will be lost but God is powerful enough to gather up all of these particles and at the Resurrection gather them together and put the clothes of a new life upon them. They interpret this as being a physical Resurrection because the return of the spirit is assured and as they are only referring to the return of the body, they have called it this.

At any rate, all of the verses of the Qur'an about the Resurrection — and these verses are many and varied — stress the physical Resurrection.

Qur'anic Proof of the Physical Resurrection

We have previously seen how a Bedouin came to the prophet with a rotten bone and asked the Prophet who would be able to enliven it. The Holy Prophet answered as God had answered,

"That very person who on the first day created them, that same person who brought the heavens and the earth into being, and Who sends out flames from the inner part of a tree. "This can be found at the end of Surah Ya Sin.

The Holy Qur'an, in another verse, says:

"You will leave your tombs at the time of the Resurrection. "(Sura Ya Sin, 36: 51 and Sura al- Qamar, 54: 7)

And we know that the grave is the place of bodies which have become dust, not the place of the spirits.

Essentially all of the surprise of those who deny the Resurrection is in this that: Once we have become dust, how is it possible that all of this dust, which has dispersed throughout the world, be gathered together and once again receive life (Sura as-Sajdah, 32:10) and the Holy Qur'an answers them that God Who created the first time has the power to do this (Sura al-"Ankabut, 29: 19)

The Bedouin had said, "Who will enliven this rotten gone?

All of these interpretations of the Qur'an and the verses show that the Prophet of Islam speaks everywhere about the physical Resurrection. The Holy Qur'an gives examples of this very physical Resurrection which takes place in world of plants and other kinds which we see. It explains it for them and brings the first creation as a witness.

Thus it is not possible that a person be a Muslim and not have the slightest knowledge of the Qur'an and the physical Resurrection and deny it because to deny the physical Resurrection from the perspective of the Qur'an, is to deny the principle of Resurrection.

Intellectual Proof

Beyond this, the intellect says that the spirit and body are two truths which are not separate from each other.

At the time of independence, the connection with each other finds nourishment with each other and they find completion and clearly require each other for the continuation of the eternal life.

Even though in the time of the intermediate world (the period between this world and the Resurrection), they are separate from each other, this is not always acceptable, just as the spirit without the body is not complete, the body without the spirit is not complete. The spirit gives the commands and is the factor for movement and without the command, and tools, there would be no command to follow or tools.

But because the spirit is at a higher level at the time of the Resurrection, its body must also be transformed and this will be. That is, the body of the human being at the time of the Resurrection will be empty of all imperfections of this world and deficiencies.

At any rate, the body and the spirit are born together and are transformed together. The Resurrection cannot have a physical or a spiritual quality.

In other words, the finding of the spirit and the body and the relation between the two of them with each other is another clear reason why the Resurrection must take place in both forms.

On the other hand, the law of justice says that the Resurrection must take place in both forms because if a human being is a sinner and the sins were committed with this body and spirit and if he or she did good deeds, it was with this body and spirit. Thus for the punishment or reward, both must be present for if only the body is present or only the spirit, justice will not be implemented.

Questions Concerning the Physical Resurrection

Scholars have expressed multiple questions on this issue which should be presented and considered.

According to the research undertaken by the natural scientists, the body of the human being in their lifetime takes on many changes or changes many times or goes through many changes. This happens every seven years in the human body. Thus throughout our lifetime, several times we change!

Now this question arises, among these changes, which form will be recreated and enlivened?

In response we say the last form. Just as we read in the above verse of the Holy Qur'an, God will transform those very bones which have rotted and become dust and this means that the last body will be returned.

But the important point is here that the last body contains all of the effects and particularities of the bodies which over time the human being has changed.

In other words, the bodies which gradually were changed will disappear, all of the special effects and particularities which exist are transferred to the next body.

Thus the last body inherits all of the qualities of this body and can, according to justice, accept punishment or rewards.

Some say that when we become dust and our dust becomes mixed with dust or fruit or trees, and as a result, we become part of the body of others, on the Day of Resurrection, what will happen.

Even though the answer to this question is very extensive, we will attempt to describe it very briefly here.

In answer to this question, we say that it is clearly the atoms which came from the dust of a person and entered the body of another which will return to the first form.

The only problem which remains is that the second body will be misshaped.

But it must be said that it will not be misshaped; it will be made smaller because all of these particles have been spread throughout the body and when taken from it, it will become smaller and thinner.

Thus neither does the first body no longer exist nor the second. The only thing which exists here is the smallness of the second body and this will not cause any problems because we know that at the time of the Resurrection, bodies of human beings will be completed and all deficiencies will be made up for in the form of new means and one's personality will not be altered. Bodies which are smaller at the Day of Judgment in the world of perfection will be considered to be perfect.

Think and Answer

1. Is the life of the human being at the time of the Resurrection similar to life in this world?

2. Can we clearly understand the rewards and punishments of the Resurrection in this world?

3. Do the punishments of hell and the rewards of heaven only have a physical quality?

4. What is meant by the embodiment of the deeds? What does the Holy Qur'an say about this?

5. What difficulties does the belief in the embodiment of the deeds in the discussion of Resurrection answer?

Lesson 50: Paradise and Hell are the Embodiment of our Deeds

Many people ask themselves, "Is the world after death similar to this world? Or does it have differences?"

Its rewards, its punishments, and, finally, the laws and system which rule it, are they like this world? In response, it must be clearly stated that: We have many witnesses in hand which show that this world and that world are very different from each other, so that that which we know in this world is like a mirage that we see from a distance.

It is best if we explain it with the example of the fetus — like the difference which exists between the world of the fetus and this world, the separation between this world and the next exists, or it is greater.

If a child who lives in the world of the fetus had intelligence and wished to have a correct image about the external world, heaven and earth, the sun and moon and stars, the mountains and jungles and seas, most certainly, it could not.

For a child who lives in the world of the fetus and who has seen nothing but the small world within its mother's womb, concepts of the moon and sun and seas and waves and thunder storms and breezes and flowers and the beauties of this world would not exist.

All of its vocabulary is summarized in a few words. And if someone outside of its mother's womb could speak with it, it would never be able to understand its language.

The limitations of this world with the extensiveness of another world is this much or more. Thus, we do not have nor will we ever have the power neither to know about the blessings of another world nor to know what Paradise is.

Thus, we read in a Tradition, "There are blessings in heaven which no eyes have seen, no ears have heard and have entered no one's brains."

The Holy Qur'an expresses this same idea in different words:

"Now no person knows what delights of the eye are kept hidden (in reserve) for them — as a reward for their good Deeds." (32:17)

The powers and systems ruling that world also have great differences with this world. For instance, in the trial of the Day of Judgment, the witnesses for the deeds of a human being will be his or her hands and feet, skin and body and even the earth upon which a sin or a good deed was performed will bear witness.

"That Day shall We set a seal on their mouths their hands will speak to Us and their feet bear witness to all that they did." (36:65)

"They, will say to their skins: "Why do you bear witness against us?" They will say, "God has given us speech — (He) Who gives speech to everything: He created you for the first time and unto Him were you to return," (41:21)

Of course, one day conceptualizing this was extremely difficult but with examples gained from the progress of science, there is no longer room for amazement.

At any rate, even though we only know the benefits of the next world as a mirage and even though we cannot come to know the extensiveness and importance and particulars of the Hereafter, but we know this much that the blessings of the world as well as its punishments are both physical and spiritual because the Resurrection contains both aspects, and, naturally, its rewards and punishments must have both aspects.

"And give glad tidings to those who believed and did good deeds that for them are gardens underneath which rivers shall flow. Wherever they are provided with a fruit from there as a provision, they shall say, "This is what we had been provided with before and shall be brought of it similarities and there, for them, are purified mates; and they are therein forever." (2:25)

"God has promised to believers, men and women, gardens under which rivers shall flow to dwell therein and beautiful mansions in gardens of everlasting bliss. But the greatest bliss is the good pleasure of God: that is the supreme felicity." (9:72)

Those who are to go to Paradise because God is satisfied with them, and their Creator has accepted them, are so happy and full of pleasure which is incomparable to anything else.

As to those who are going to go to Hell, in addition to the fire and harsh physical punishments, the anger of the Creator is awaiting them, and that is greater than any kind of torture.

Embodiment of Deeds

It is worth noting that many verses of the Holy Qur'an can be used to show that at the Resurrection, our deeds will be enlivened and will be present for us in various ways and one of the important areas of rewards and punishments is this very embodiment of deeds.

Oppression and injustice will appear in the form of black tools and will surround us as a Tradition from the Holy Prophet tells us, "Injustice is darkness on the Day of Resurrection."

"They will soon be enduring a blazing fire." (4:10)

"One Day shall you see the believing men and the believing women, how their light runs forward before them and by their right hands (their greeting will be), "Good News for you this Day! Gardens beneath which flows rivers! To dwell therein forever. This is indeed the highest achievement." (57:12)

"And let not those who covetously withhold of the gifts which God has given them of His Grace, think that it is good for them. Nay, it will be the worse for them. Soon shall the things which they covetously withheld be tied to their necks like a twisted collar on the Day of Judgment to God belongs the heritage of the heavens and the earth." (3:180)

We know that knowledge and science today tells us that nothing in the world is destroyed; material and energy are continuously changing form without them ever disappearing. Our deeds and acts are no different and according to this rule, they remain eternally, The Holy Qur'an, in a short and strong sentence, says about the Resurrection,

"And the Book (of Deeds) will be placed (before you); and you will see the sinful in great terror because of what is (recorded) therein; they will say, "O! Woe be upon us! What a book this is! It, leaves out nothing, small or great, but takes account thereof!" They will find all that they did, placed before them; and not one will your Lord treat with injustice. "Behold! We said to the angels, "Bow down to Adam, they bowed except Iblis. He was one of the jinns and he broke the command of his Lord. Will you then take him and his progeny as protectors rather than Me? And they are enemies to you!" (18:49-50)

"On that Day will men proceed in companies sorted out to be shown the deeds that they (had done)." (99:6)

"So, he who has done an atom"s weight of good shall see it...And he who has done an atom"s weight of evil shall see it." (99:7)

Notice that it says you will see that very deed.

The fact that our deeds, large and small, good and bad, will remain guarded and permanent in this world and will not be destroyed and at the Day of Judgment, they will be with us, can be a warning to all so that we stand up before ugliness and evil and a corrupt environment and be loyal and desirous of good deeds.

The amazing thing is that today, things have been invented which can help us envision this fact in this world.

At any rate, many of the questions which relate to the Resurrection and the eternality of rewards for good deeds and punishments for evil deeds in the Holy Qur'an refers to good or bad deeds in our spirit and body which leave effects and these effects will always remain with us.

Think and Answer

1. Is the life of the human being at the Resurrection exactly similar to life in this world?

2. Can we really conceive of rewards and punishments of the Resurrection?

3. Do the rewards for good deeds and punishments for evil deeds only have a physical quality?

4. What does embodiment of deeds mean and how does the Holy Qur'an refer to it?

5. At the Resurrection, what difficulty does "embodiment of deeds' solve?

www.ingramcontent.com/pod-product-compliance
Lightning Source LLC
Chambersburg PA
CBHW021438070526
44577CB00002B/207